To Esther + Bob,

mentors to many.

God bless you in your

life together.

HUME LAKE

The
FineArt
of
Mentoring

The FINE ART of MENTORING

Passing On To Others
What God Has Given To You

Ted W. Engstrom
with Norman B. Rohrer

Wolgemuth & Hyatt, Publishers, Inc.
Brentwood, Tennessee

The mission of Wolgemuth & Hyatt, Publishers, Inc. is to publish and distribute books that lead individuals toward:

- A personal faith in the one true God: Father, Son, and Holy Spirit;

- A lifestyle of practical discipleship; and

- A worldview that is consistent with the historic, Christian faith.

Moreover, the Company endeavors to accomplish this mission at a reasonable profit and in a manner which glorifies God and serves His Kingdom.

Unless otherwise noted, all scripture quotations are from the Holy Bible, New International Version. © 1973, 1978, 1984 International Bible Society. Used by permission of Zondervan Bible Publishers.

Wolgemuth & Hyatt, Publishers, Inc.
1749 Mallory Lane, Suite 110, Brentwood, Tennessee 37027.

Library of Congress Cataloging-in-Publication Data

Engstrom, Theodore Wilhelm, 1916–
    The fine art of mentoring : passing on to others what God has given you / Ted W. Engstrom with Norman B. Rohrer.
        p. cm.
    Includes bibliographical references.
    ISBN 0-943497-63-9 : $13.95
    1. Witness bearing (Chrisitianity) 2. Christian education.
I. Rohrer, Norman B. II. Title.
BV4520.E54   1989
253.7 — dc20   89-28094
                                                                CIP

With affection—
To those who mentored me
and to those whom I've had
the delightful privilege
of mentoring

CONTENTS

FOREWORD

I have a hunch that a book on mentoring would not have been necessary one hundred years ago, and an eighteenth century publisher might have muttered irreverently, "What's the fuss all about?" That's because, up until recently, mentoring—the development of a person—was a way of life between the generations. It was to human relationships what breathing is to the body. Mentoring was assumed, expected, and, therefore, almost unnoticed because of its commonness in human experience.

In the past, mentoring happened everywhere. On the farm, a boy or a girl was mentored along side of mothers, fathers, and extended family members. From the earliest years, these mentors gave children a sense of "maleness" and "femaleness" and taught them what work was all about and how it was done, what character meant, and what were the duties and obligations of each member of the community.

Mentoring was the chief learning method in the society of artisans where an apprentice spent years at the side of the craftsman learning not only the mechanics of a function, but the "way of life" which surrounded it. A similar pattern was pursued in the old university where a student learned in the home of the scholar; it occurred in the old royal court where the knight imparted the warrior's skills to the novice and in the studio where the artist poured himself into the formation of his protégés. In the world of spiritual development, the mentoring pattern was universal. Eighteenth century New England pastor and wife, Jonathan and Sarah Edwards, usually had one or more "disciples" living in their home where there was ample time for the learner to observe the quality of a marriage, personal spiritual dynamics, and the vigorous pursuit of pastoral activity.

In contrast to the past, the mentoring function today is in short supply. It is certainly not found in those homes where children part company with their parents for the better part of each day and accumulate an average of only eight to eleven minutes of parent-child conversation before the sun sets. And it is not found on most campuses where faculty and students rarely meet outside the class room. Nor is it found in many parts of industry where the craftsman has given ground to the technician. If mentoring has survived, you'll see it best in the world of athletics and the arts where outstanding performance can only be developed through individual, one-on-one encounters.

Today, what passes for people development happens in a class room, and the certification of a person is by diploma from an institution rather than the stamp of approval from an overseer, a mentor. The criteria for the judgment of people usually rests upon knowledge rather than wisdom, achievement rather than character, profit rather than creativity. And as long as that is true, mentoring will likely be a second class matter in our value system.

But the good news is that more than a few are waking up to the fact that we have lost something precious in our culture because the mentoring function has been permitted to lapse into semi-obsolescence. There is a renewal of reference to mentoring in the business literature, the world of education, and in social work. And that new alertness has been in evidence of course in the Christ-following community also. Some are newly discovering that virtually all training of the people of the Bible happened in the mentoring context. Others are learning that preaching and acquisition of Biblical knowledge is not enough to develop the sort of Christ-likeness which is a major segment of the Church's mission in the world.

And that's why a twentieth century publisher would most likely seize an opportunity to present the reading public with a good book on mentoring even if an eighteenth century publisher might be tempted to pass it by. He would understand our desperate need to recover the mentoring function and make it the prime activity in all human relationships.

It's also why I'm so delighted that the twentieth century publisher of this book has given me the privilege of introducing it. I believe strongly in the topic, and my belief is based upon my own personal experience of being a mentor and of being mentored. It is also based upon my awareness that the Bible urges this kind of intersection between the spiritual generations. And, finally, it's based on my observation that Jesus spent far more time developing a few teachable people than he did dazzling the crowds with words.

It is fitting that Ted Engstrom has addressed the topic of mentoring, and I'm delighted that he chose to write about mentoring and not about discipleship. For much of the emphasis on what is called discipleship in Christian circles (while helpful) has tended to center on a rather narrow segment of personal spirituality: Bible study, spiritual growth, and the enhancement of the spiritual gifts. But my special friend, Ted, has reminded us that the development of people (for that is what mentoring is) is much more holistic. It includes the "sculpting" of people-values, the shaping of response patterns to crisis and opportunity, the acquisition of habits of work, the enlargement of one's hunger for God, and the expansion of our view of creation. And much more!

I started to say that it's fitting for Ted Engstrom to write this book because of at least two things. First, he has done the mentoring he writes about. Men and women all over the world will gladly and thankfully attest to that. And secondly, he writes from the perspective of a generation which is in the process of handing its work over to successors. As a friend and one-time member of the board of World Vision/United States, I've been in a position to see Ted do both, and he has done it and continues to do it well. So while the material in this book ranges far and wide across the centuries and across the world of faith, it is all grounded in the accumulated activities of a man who gave his life to managing resources and building people.

The mentoring leader (and that is what Ted Engstrom has been) is a scarce human commodity. So I commend to you the thoughts of one of those wonderful rarities: a Christlike man who has produced Christlike protégés.

Gordon MacDonald
New York City

"Come to the edge," he said.
They said, "We are afraid."
"Come to the edge," he said.
They came.
He pushed them . . . and they flew.

Guillaume Apollinaire

INTRODUCTION

S uccessful people never reach their goals alone. Standing with them is a contingent of resourceful counselors in a network of relationships. Among them are what Judy Viorst calls (1) convenience friends, (2) special-interest friends, (3) historical friends, (4) crossroad friends, (5) cross-generational friends, and (6) close friends.[1] This book introduces a fascinating seventh category that encompasses them all yet stands in a classification apart.

The term "mentor," a catchword surfacing in discussions about leadership development today, arises from an unlikely source. It first appeared in Greek mythology when Ulysses asked a wise man named Mentor in Homer's *Odyssey* to care for his son, Telemachus, while Ulysses was fighting in the Trojan War. Mentor taught the boy "not only in book learning but also in the wiles of the world." To be sure, the original Mentor had an unfair advantage over his namesakes today. Whenever his duties demanded more than he could handle, the goddess Athena mysteriously appeared, took on his form and lent a hand. The fabled Mentor must have done his job well, because Telemachus grew up to be an enterprising lad who gallantly helped his father recover his kingdom.

For the Christian, "mentoring" has objectives in the real world that are beyond the stuff of legends. "Discipling" is a close synonym, with these differences: A discipler is one who helps an understudy to (1) give up his own will for the will of God the Father, (2) live daily a life of spiritual sacrifice for the glory of Christ, and (3) strive to be consistently obedient to the commands of his Master. A mentor, on the other hand, provides modeling, close supervision on special projects, individualized help in many areas — discipline, encouragement, correction, confrontation, and a calling to accountability.

Chris Adsit, author of *Personal Disciplemaking* (Here's Life Publishers, 1988), sees mentoring as "a subset of disciplemaking." Discipleship takes in the entire scope of what happens when a Christian cooperates with the Holy Spirit to create an environment in which a younger Christian can grow. Mentoring is a broader term describing the process of developing a man or a woman to his or her maximum potential in Jesus Christ in every vocation.

Generally speaking, a mentor

- is a person who has achieved superior rank on an organizational or professional ladder.

- is an authority in his or her field as the result of disciplined work, study, and experience.

- has a certain measure of influence in his or her chosen field.

- is genuinely interested in a protégé's growth and development.

- is willing to commit time and emotional energy to a relationship with an understudy. This goes beyond mere interest and is a commitment that, more often than not, is intense.

On the other hand, there are some things that a mentor is not: He is not

- automatically a pal or a buddy, or one to be included necessarily in family gatherings or other social functions.

- "on call" for grievances and frustrations, imagined or real. A good mentor may well have more than one mentoree (or protégé), so his time should be limited to discussions about major opportunities, problems, and tactics, not minor ones.

- to be gracefully dismissed when the mentoree decides that the relationship is no longer useful. The association has a natural cycle of its own — not a predictable span of time but a function of individual growth adapting to changing circumstances.

To the Christian believer, there is no greater "mentor" than Jesus Christ the Lord. How He fashioned His meek-spirited followers into an invincible company of overcomers is a display of divine mentoring to which we humans can only aspire. Nevertheless, the mentoring of the Master in this book will be a touchstone and the measure of a mentor in our world today.

Moses taught Joshua, Naomi taught Ruth, Elijah taught Elisha, Elizabeth taught Mary, Barnabas taught Paul, Paul taught Timothy, Priscilla and Aquila taught Apollos. . . .

Now that we know what to call it, whom are you mentoring today?

Be what you would have your pupils to be.

Thomas Carlyle

ONE

PORTRAIT OF
A MENTOR

*[Barnabas] encouraged them all to remain true to the
Lord with all their hearts. He was a good man, full of
the Holy Spirit and faith.*

Acts 11:23, 24

The hoary mists of time roll away and the city of Jerusalem appears. Thousands of Jews are pouring through the narrow streets, jamming the concourses, and overflowing the synagogues for the fifty-day celebration of Pentecost. From the Parthian Empire they come and from Media, Elam, Judea, Cappadocia, Pontus, Asia, Phrygia, Pamphylia, Egypt, and Rome—all Jews but struggling to communicate in an array of languages as they buy food, pick through souvenirs, and intone their prayers. They've saved their money for the event and intend to make the most of the celebration. Sunrise, sunset . . . sunrise, sunset . . . and the Feast of Harvest grinds on.

In the upper room of an obscure house, eleven men, including the apostle newly elected to take the place of Judas "who left to go where he belongs," are kneeling in prayer. A faint rustle of wind interrupts their prayers. It quickly fills the house and spirals into a roaring torch, then separates into flames of fire that rest on each of the twelve men. The wind roars out through the windows and doors to the city beyond, and is replaced by the sound of the apostles speaking in many languages as the Holy Spirit gave them utterance.

As the apostles rush into the street, declaring the good news that the Holy Spirit has come, thousands of faithful Jews embrace the gospel of the risen Christ. And thousands go to their rooms, unpack their bags, cancel plans to return home, and settle in to see what will happen next. Historians calculate that the Church grew to one hundred thousand members in just a few weeks.

One of the Jews who remained in Jerusalem was a Levite from Cyprus named Joseph. This faithful believer quickly realized that funds would be needed to feed the new believers and to sustain the work of evangelism to which the apostles were dramatically committed. Without hesitation, the Cypriot merchant sold some of his property and laid the money at the apostles' feet. What joy! The apostles jubilantly changed his name from Joseph the Levite to Barnabas ("Son of Encouragement").

Do you want to be a mentor? Be generous.

The Church grew fast and jealousy followed right behind. Religious leaders were outraged by the New Way. An intense rabbi named Saul, breathing out threats against the followers of Jesus Christ, supervised the stoning of Stephen. Then, with letters of authorization in his pocket, he took the Damascus Road and ran straight into the arms of Jesus.

When word reached the ears of the apostles that Saul of Tarsus claimed to be a believer, they were suspicious. "This murderer is faking it," they said. "It's his subversive trick to get inside the Church."

When Saul arrived in Jerusalem from Damascus, Barnabas met him and provided for his needs. "Saul has seen the Lord," Barnabas told the apostles. "In Damascus he preached the gospel fearlessly. This one is for real."

Do you want to be a mentor? Believe in people. Take time to know them and help to meet their needs.

It was soon time to take the gospel to other cities. Barnabas suggested that he and Paul take John Mark with them, but Paul was adamantly opposed. Barnabas was willing to risk his relationship with the apostle by standing firm for John Mark. "Sorry, Paul," he said. "I'm not going to let you do that to this young man. You'll wipe him out."

Do you want to be a mentor? Stand up for your friends. Don't let them be destroyed by discouragement.

The question of association with Grecian Jews surfaced in Jerusalem. Paul was away; Peter was still in process and couldn't handle the assignment; Judaizers in the church were unprepared for the debates. Barnabas had no prejudice. The Son of Encouragement happily volunteered. And when he got to Jerusalem, he was *glad*. He was *excited* by the work of God in their midst.

Do you want to be a mentor? Then get excited about the good things that happen in the lives of others.

Before Pentecost, when the apostles cast lots to fill the vacancy left by the death of Judas, the lot fell upon Matthias. The one who lost was Joseph called Barsabas.

Joseph was called but not elected to become the twelfth apostle. Did he pout? Did he feel hurt, retreat and lick his wounds? Not for a moment. If my thesis is correct that Joseph the Levite, Barnabas himself, is indeed the one who lost, then it's easy to see why he fought so hard for the underdog. Why did he sell his property and give it to the struggling Church? Why did he step in when every other believer was suspicious of Saul? Why did he risk the success of a missionary trip with the unpopular John Mark? Why did he try to unite the squabbling Jews and Christians in Jerusalem? He did so because he knew what it was like being on the outside looking in.

Do you want to be a mentor? Then seek to affirm others and encourage them in their walk with the Lord.

Joseph's name was changed to "Son of Encouragement" to match his character. If someone changed your name to correspond to your lifestyle, what would they call you?

I hope they would call you "Mentor."

Leadership is both something you *are* and something you *do*. A mentor is not a person who can do the work better than his followers; he is a person who can get his followers to do the work better than he can.

Fred Smith

T W O

ANYONE CAN /
EVERYONE SHOULD

*We loved you so much that we were delighted to share
with you not only the gospel of God but our lives as
well. . . .*

1 Thessalonians 2:8

E arly one morning in a crowded elevator, a businessman
became annoyed by another's cheerfulness. "What are
you so happy about?" he growled.

"Well, sir, I ain't never lived this day before!" came
the reply.[1]

No one else in the elevator had either, but the one
who had the optimism and perception to see the possibilities
of the new day became, for a brief moment, a mentor
to the rest. Such quality of life cannot be taught, only
caught.

Frank Lloyd Wright had it. At the age of eighty-three he was asked which of his architectural works he would select as his most important. He replied, "The next one."[2]

Viktor Frankl, who spent years in a concentration camp, had it. He noticed that those who believed in tomorrow best survived the day. Those who believed that tomorrow would never come were those who could not survive:

> The prisoner who had lost his faith in the future — his future — was doomed. With his loss of belief in the future, he also lost his spiritual hold; he let himself decline and become subject to mental and physical decay.[3]

Lee Iaccoca, head of the Chrysler Corporation, had it. He expressed this view of the future beautifully:

> It's a good thing God doesn't let you look a year or two into the future, or you might be sorely tempted to shoot yourself. But he's a charitable Lord: He only lets you see one day at a time. When times get tough, there's no choice except to take a deep breath, carry on, and do the best you can.[4]

D. Elton Trueblood, Quaker philosopher and long-time professor at Earlham College and Seminary, had it. His method of teaching was intense. After meeting J. Keith Miller at Laity Lodge in the Texas hill country, he took the bright young man and "force-fed" him the Christian classics. Later, Dr. Trueblood invited him to be Guest Lecturer at Earlham Theological Seminary in Richmond, Indiana. I had the privilege of editing Keith's book, *The Taste of New Wine*, published by Word Books, which grew out of this mentoring. Of his experience with his mentor, Keith Miller recalls:

> Elton's technique was very direct. For example, when I was a student, he put me in a senior seminar made up of top-notch philosophy majors. The seminar was on the work of that very complex philosopher, Alfred North Whitehead. I had never had a course in philosophy. Something came up about "Plato's receptacle." I asked what that was. Elton was horrified and handed me the complete dialogues of Plato right then (on a Friday morning) and said he wanted me to read them before Monday. As I recall, I did — by staying up most of the nights. He kept doing that to me until I understood whatever subject was discussed. It was terrible and wonderful and made me realize how much I could learn in a hurry by paying the price to get the material.[5]

Anne Mansfield Sullivan had it. A classic example of a mentor/teacher, she was engaged by the parents of Helen Keller to teach their blind and deaf seven-year-old child. On March 3, 1887 in Tuscumbia, northern Alabama, she began her mission that would astonish the world. On March 20, 1887, Miss Sullivan wrote:

> My heart is singing for joy this morning. A miracle has happened! The light of understanding has shone upon my little pupil's mind, and behold, all things are changed.

> The wild little creature of two weeks ago has been transformed into a gentle child. She is sitting by me as I write, her face serene and happy, crocheting a long red chain of Scotch wool.[6]

Mary Kay Ash had it. After retirement she started a cosmetic sales firm that became a $300 million company within two decades with hundreds of protégés, many of them earning as much as $50,000 a year. She did it with the belief that "the Golden Rule is intended to be used seven days a week—not just on Sunday—and should be employed in every relationship—business and personal."[7]

Even Ebenezer Scrooge, in Charles Dickens' *A Christmas Carol*, finally had it. "Mentored" by Jacob Marley's ghost, by Bob Cratchit, and by Tiny Tim, the miserly old gent of the classic exclaimed at last, "I will not be the man I was."

LeRoy Eims and some fellow members of The Navigators have it. During World War II in the South Pacific, they sought out a Marine from Houston, Texas, eight thousand miles away from home. Charles R. Swindoll had formed a habit of memorizing verses of Scripture, but his view of the Christian world was restricted to the little church of his childhood in Texas far away.

"One day, a member of The Navigators tapped me on the shoulder and everything changed," Chuck said. "I was awestruck when he showed me the emptiness of my faith. He took away the small tube through which I looked at life and showed me that there was much more God had for me."

Chuck Swindoll went on to become pastor of The Evangelical Free Church in Fullerton, California, a radio speaker heard daily on hundreds of stations, and the author of scores of best-selling books.

Henrietta Mears had it. The wealthy, fashionable Minneapolis schoolteacher and administrator, holder of a doctorate in science, became the visionary founder of Gospel Light Publications during her stint as Christian

Education Director at the First Presbyterian Church of Hollywood a generation ago. Dr. Mears saw her efforts help make "Hollywood Pres" the largest and most effective Presbyterian church in the world. Her dynamism and approachability drew movie stars to her spacious home in Coldwater Canyon for counsel and help. She mentored hundreds of young candidates for the Christian ministry and was the driving force behind the purchase of the Forest Home Christian Conference Center in the San Bernardino Mountains of Southern California. Billy Graham called her "one of the greatest Christians I've ever known."

Donald Grey Barnhouse, pastor for decades of Tenth Presbyterian Church in Philadelphia, had it. He could read the scriptures in German and French, sampling also the Hebrew and Greek texts of the original sacred writings in his long hours of study. He told his colleague, Russell T. Hitt: "Don't cut yourself off from your unbelieving friends. Most Christians live largely in their Christian ghettos and speak their own jargon. Few of them know how to relate to unbelievers."

Edward B. "Ted" Cole had it. Pastor for twenty-eight years of the First Baptist Church of Pomona, California, he was mentor to a total of 280 young men and women whom he groomed for the ministry. His church was the American Baptist Convention's largest congregation and a church which sponsored eleven other congregations throughout Southern California.

His mother, Bible teacher Genevieve Bender Cole (who was the wife of a man in the lumber business), also had it. For several decades she had taught three Bible classes for women in Los Angeles, Glendale, and Pasadena, California. In her inimitable, infectious manner, she conveyed to her listeners the joy, attractiveness, and balance of the Christian life.

Fred Smith, president of Fred Smith Associates, a Dallas-based food packaging company, calls mentoring both "instruction" and "coaching."

> Instruction is what Plato referred to as transferring information from one mind to the other. Much of the technology information can be transferred by instructors. Instruction deals with how to do something useful—something for which one has a talent and something one can swap in the market for financial return and recognition as a craftsman. Coaching, on the other hand, is the process of developing unique qualities in the art of learning. For example, such things as thinking, feeling, and dedication to excellence cannot be given by instruction—they can only be developed by coaching/mentoring.[8]

In New Hampshire's Franconia Notch State Park, one can look with wonder at the Great Stone Face. When I recall Nathaniel Hawthorne's story, "The Great Stone Face," I am intrigued by the devotion of young Ernest, the main character, to that outcropping of rock in the White Mountains.

In Hawthorne's story, Ernest's face gradually took on the features of that old man as he gazed at him day after day. Many men had come, claiming to be the fulfillment of a prophecy that a child would be born "hereabouts" who was destined to become "the greatest and noblest personage of his time." None could qualify—not Mr. Gathergold, not Old Blood-and-Thunder, and not Old Stony Phiz. It was Ernest himself, the poet, who became the likeness of the Great Stone Face because he had looked upon it so long and with such utter devotion.

There is another face, another Person, more worthy of our gaze as the years of our lives pass. All who would become like Jesus must look continually upon the face of our supreme Mentor and guide, with a willingness to obey His commands.

Three Models

Every Christian mentor needs a Barnabas to receive encouragement, a Timothy to guide as a protégé, and an Epaphraditus to enjoy on a peer level. My "Barnabas" has been Carlton Booth, with whom I've worked for a quarter of a century. When I've faced difficult decisions, Carlton was always there with an encouraging word. When plans have not turned out as intended, Carlton knew how to find the bright side and would often suggest that we pray together to find God's will in a matter.

My "Timothy" has been a host of young men. One of my closest was Bill Kliewer, for more than twenty years an executive director under me and a man in whom I've invested hours, weeks, and months of time with great joy.

My "Epaphraditus" has been Jay Kesler; my pastor, Paul Cedar; along with Bob Cook; and many, many other men who are not so well-known. Work, leisure, and worship knit our hearts together in the bonds of Christ.

It is certainly true that the mentor gains as much personal benefit from the mentoring relationship as the protégé. For the mentoree, personal satisfaction and career development are natural outcomes of fulfilling one's potential. The mentor, on the other hand, derives immeasurable satisfaction from having assisted another on a long-term, permanent basis.

The Apostle Paul in 2 Timothy 2:3 instructs his protégé to "endure hardship with us like a good soldier of Christ Jesus." In verse five, he challenges his mentoree to "compete as an athlete" according to the rules, with a view to winning the victor's crown.

And finally in verse six, Paul reminds Timothy that as he serves in the Lord's army and competes like an athlete, he will be like the hard-working farmer who enjoys the first fruits of his harvest.

When my pastor, Paul Cedar of the Lake Avenue Congregational Church in Pasadena, California, was starting out in the ministry, he took a position as Crusade Director with the Billy Graham Evangelistic Association. One day in Omaha, Nebraska where Paul was helping to lay the groundwork for a crusade, the distinguished pastor of a large Lutheran congregation of several thousand people came to see him. This is the discovery the senior pastor shared with Paul:

One day a young man dropped in to see his pastor and told him about a co-worker at the plant whose life was a mess. "Would you be willing to talk to him, pastor?" he asked.

"Yes, of course. I'll be happy to talk to him."

The pastor had lunch with the troubled co-worker and found him quite open to the gospel.

Weeks went by and the concerned friend again visited the pastor. "The man you had lunch with is in dire need again," he reported. "Would you be willing to see him?"

Then a light came on in the head of the pastor. He asked the young man, "How well do you know your co-worker?"

"Oh," he replied, "I know him very, very well. We've worked together for many years. In fact, we ride together to work and eat lunch together nearly every day."

Now his idea grew more intense. "You know," the pastor said, "I may be able to see your friend once in a while but you're with him every day—week after week. Wouldn't it be a much better strategy for me to train you so that you could teach him about Christ?"

That was a radical thought to a congregation that hired clergy to "do ministry." The layman was willing to become a mentor to his fellow worker and out of that came good things for Christ and His Kingdom.

Mentors worth their title will show a protégé how to work while others waste time, how to study while others procrastinate, and how to pray while others play.

Joshua set a good example for all who would be mentors. His mentor, Moses, spoke with the Lord "face to face, as a man speaks with his friend," and Joshua, Moses' young aide, "did not leave [Moses'] tent" (Exodus 33:11).

My friend Paul Borthwick tells the story of Don, a corporate executive with an ITT company, who was known by associates for his Christian character. Paul asked him how he had developed as a Christian leader in a competitive environment. He explained it in one sentence: "I chose a good mentor." His mentor exemplified Christian character in the business world, and Don developed his own leadership style around that example.[9]

The poet Henry Wadsworth Longfellow might have been thinking of mentors when he wrote:

> The heights by great men reached and kept
> Were not attained by sudden flight,
> But they, while their companions slept,
> Were toiling upward in the night.

Steps to Effective Mentoring

To be effective in the role of a mentor and to enjoy your experiences, take these steps:

1. Select a mentoree whose philosophy of life you share. Our greatest mentors are those who are also our models.

2. Choose a person with potential you genuinely believe in. Some of the nation's greatest athletes have come from tiny schools that receive no publicity. All those ball players needed was for scouts to recognize the potential that great coaching could bring out. The secret of mentoring in any field is to help a person get to where he or she is willing to go.

3. Evaluate a mentoree's progress constantly. An honest mentor will be objective. If necessary, he or she will encourage the person to stay on course, to seek another direction, or even to enter into a relationship with another mentor.

4. Be committed, serious, and available to mentorees. New York Philharmonic Conductor Zubin Mehta said of a young pianist: "I cannot teach him how to play, for he knows what the composer wanted to say; I can simply help him say it."

Every mentor should also have a mentor. To choose the best:

1. Ask him or her to help you ask the right questions, search in the right places, and stay interested in the right answers.

2. Decide what degree of excellence or perfection you want. Generally the object of mentoring is improvement, not perfection. Perhaps only a few can be truly excellent — but all can be better.

3. Accept a subordinate, learning position. Don't let ego get in the way of learning or try to impress the mentor with your knowledge or ability and thus set up a mental barrier against taking in as fast as it's being given out.

4. Respect the mentor but don't idolize him. Respect allows us to accept what he or she is teaching — but making the mentor an idol removes our critical faculty for fitting a mentor's thinking to ourselves.

5. Put into effect immediately what you are learning. The best mentoring is intensity in a narrow field. Learn, practice, and assimilate.

6. Set up a discipline for relating to the mentor. Arrange for an ample and consistent time schedule, select the subject matter in advance, and do your homework to make the sessions profitable.

7. Reward your mentor with your own progress. If you show appreciation but make no progress, the mentor knows he's failed. Your progress is his highest reward.

8. Learn to ask crucial questions — questions that prove you have been thinking between sessions, questions that show progress in your perception.

9. Don't threaten to give up. Let your mentor know that you have made a decision for progress, that

he is dealing with a persistent person — a determined winner. Then he knows he is not wasting
his time.

A good mentor will notice any hesitation, nervous-
ness, or indecision and find the cause of this lack of poise.
We cannot hide if we are to be helped.

Do your best as mentor and protégé to make the time
count. Even the longest life is but a vapor that appears for
a short time then vanishes away. And when all of life is
over and we reach the other side, everything but the
Kingdom of God will be irrelevant. The only thing that
will matter is whether we have done the will of God.

The Ten Commandments of Mentoring

1. Thou shalt not play God.

2. Thou shalt not play Teacher.

3. Thou shalt not play Mother or Father.

4. Thou shall not lie with your body.

5. Active listening is the holy time and thou shalt practice it at every session.

6. Thou shalt be nonjudgmental.

7. Thou shalt not lose heart because of repeated disappointments.

8. Thou shalt practice empathy, not sympathy.

9. Thou shalt not believe that thou can move mountains.

10. Thou shalt not envy thy neighbor's protégé, nor thy neighbor's success.

John C. Crosby
The Uncommon Individual Foundation

THREE

CALLING PROTÉGÉS TO ACCOUNT

Nothing in all creation is hidden from God's sight. Everything is uncovered and laid bare before the eyes of Him to whom we must give account.

Hebrews 4:13

I n the past half century, I have traveled literally millions of miles and visited 135 countries. Everywhere I go people ask me, "Whom can I trust? Are there any good guys anymore? Is everybody out only for the dollar? Are there any normal families? Is anybody held accountable anymore for their actions?" Maybe I've overemphasized the point, but basically these are the kinds of questions people are asking.

Most people have no argument about being accountable to God. He is our Father; He is perfect; He has every right to check up on us to see if we are on course. But when we think of giving an account to anyone here on

29

earth, that can be a touchy matter. Those independent types who are self-made men and women find it especially hard to bare their souls to a self-appointed overseer.

Because it is so awkward, it is rare today when anyone calls another to account for his deeds. However, calling someone to account is an act of love beautifully suited to a mentor. No one can ask the hard questions and demand answers as effectively as a trusted mentor. Forcing a mentoree to open his life to a confidant who has earned the right to be heard can save marriages from divorce, churches from division, organizations from financial disaster, and careers from ruin.

Why is this dramatic and important matter so rarely discussed among friends? Insurance companies do not hesitate to call a client into account. A bank or trust company certainly will do it. So will employment agencies, military recruiters, accredited academic institutions, and law enforcement agencies. Why not the church? Why not a friend?

As an example, a mentor must first be accountable himself. This means he must be vulnerable and not hesitate to show weakness or to admit that he's wrong. A mentor responds quickly to reproof and sets an example by seeking direction. A mentor lives not to himself but is open, accessible, touchable, interruptible. Telling the truth is not a problem to seasoned mentors no matter how much it hurts.

When a mentor is forced to assess the action of his friend, it must not be idle gossip. It must not be probing for personal reasons. He should be persistent until the mentoree listens to the counsel and takes action to remedy the situation.

I've had people express gratitude for reproof. I've also had friends resist and be so offended at my remarks that they have turned and walked away before I was finished talking. I've had people argue with me.

One day an employee came into my office with a serious complaint about a fellow worker, which I knew was not a legitimate one. I sought to counsel him that such gossip was harmful and would do no one any good. He was so distressed with my word to him, which I felt was necessary, that he stormed out of the office and told all who would listen that I was most unreasonable and would not take the action proposed. This incident, and his response, caused such unrest among our people that I had to release him, unfortunately, from his responsibilities. He simply refused to accept being accountable for spreading harmful gossip.

Stages of Accountability

As children grow and mature, they often step away from one of the healthiest situations their lives will ever enjoy — the accountability they had with mom and dad. Just as they reach the critical years of the late teens and early twenties, the young people move into a dormitory or get a job in another part of the country, or marry and move in with a mate. By now the relationship of accountability at home is nearly gone.

Mother and father don't say much, even though they see their children making unwise decisions, lest they appear to be meddling and keeping the children dependent. Young people risk abusing their power unless a mentor is there who loves them enough to tell them the truth.

Or perhaps the kids are beginning to make money, and there is no one around to offer counsel on how to spend it and save it wisely, unless a mentor loves them enough to give them guidance.

And far too often the marriage shows signs of strain that may lead to a breakdown, unless a mentor loves them enough to tell them the truth.

Promotions move people into situations that offer just enough power for persons to hang themselves, unless a mentor tells them the truth in love.

Accountability in the Bible

When Joseph was in the house of Potiphar, he was accountable to him. Even when Potiphar's wife made those unwise advances on the innocent man and later screamed rape, Joseph was accountable to Potiphar.

When Saul became king, he was in a hurry for the prophet Samuel to arrive so an offering could be made. Samuel was late, so Saul took matters into his own hands. He gathered together an offering, and *he* presented it to the Lord. When Samuel arrived, he rebuked the king of Israel because Saul the king was accountable to Samuel the prophet.

When David scandalized the nation by committing adultery with Bathsheba and by murdering Uriah, Nathan the prophet stood before the king of the nation and charged him with the crimes because David the king was accountable to Nathan the prophet.

When Nehemiah wanted to travel to Jerusalem and rebuild the city wall, he had to get permission from Artaxerxes because he was accountable to the king for whom he worked as a cupbearer.

When Daniel had to disobey the king and his colleagues, he remained very much at ease, because he was accountable to God and there was nothing to hide.

One of the things that marked the life of our Lord when He came to earth was His submission to the Father's will. The Apostle John tells us on more than one occasion, "Jesus always did the things that pleased the Father."

To the twelve men whom Jesus had selected to be His disciples He passed the torch for the work of the ministry. These men were accountable to Him and, ultimately, to each other.

Paul and Silas were accountable to the church at Antioch — Onesimus, the slave, was accountable to Philemon — Timothy was accountable to Paul because the apostle was his father in the faith.

A Mentor's Strategy

Mentors need wisdom from above to keep a mentoree accountable in the many and varied problems that are sure to surface. Sometimes an objective opinion will reveal a blind spot in the life of a friend. Sometimes a straight-from-the-shoulder bit of advice will work. Strong reproof will often get a mistaken and/or wayward person back on track. And sometimes a mentor provides a sounding board to listen while a friend puts himself back on target.

I've noticed that behavior put under close scrutiny tends to change for the better. People who are made accountable to a mentor, to a group of friends, to a therapy group, to a psychiatrist, to a pastoral counselor, or to a prayer group become serious about changing their behavior.

Studies carried out in factories involving hundreds of employees have proven that both the quality and the quantity of work increase when employees know they are being observed and will be called to account for the work they do. If God alone is witness, the person far too often unfortunately tends to make all kinds of excuses. But if that same person must report to peers, he begins to monitor his behavior and improve it.

In times of trouble, a mentor might be called upon merely to listen, to offer a word of advice, and not infrequently to confront the individual with words of rebuke. When there is improvement, invariably it means that the person has been called to account. An unaccountable spouse is living on the edge of risk; an unaccountable CEO is in danger of taking his company down a wrong road; an unaccountable pastor has too much authority; an unaccountable counselor has too much responsibility and needs too much wisdom to be able to handle it on his own.

The mentor who sees his charge stumble must invade that person's private world. Change will most likely never happen unless that is done.

The classic example of a leader who went wild with authority is Jim Jones. The Jonestown carnage was the tragic result.

For many years I deliberately chose to be accountable to a group of five other men with whom I formed a breakfast fellowship. We met together twice a month simply to share with each other. This was not a Bible study or a prayer time, but simply regularly scheduled occasions to relate to each other and to seek to be accountable to one another spiritually. We would discuss for an hour and a half or so a host of subjects — sports, politics, business, church — but always seek to minister to each other and be accountable to the others related to our walk with God. I knew that these were men who willingly held me spiritually responsible, and I them. It proved to be, for a dozen or more years, a most helpful and redemptive experience for each of us to recognize this accountability factor in our lives.

The best mentor also has a mentor. Are *you* accountable to someone outside your family? To someone who can ask hard questions and expect honest answers? To someone to whom you make yourself available so that you can look at your life critically? If such activity is threatening, then you have the wrong mentors. Some people, of course, will be only too happy to make the world accountable to them. They would not hesitate to tell you all the wrong things in your life. They have the gift of criticism, and they will be happy to exercise it on your behalf.

That's not the type you need. I'm talking about people who love you too much to let you play with fire . . . people who are concerned enough about you to be hard on you when you need it. The Book of Proverbs says it well:

Wisdom is found in those who take advice. (Proverbs 13:10)

The teaching of the wise is a fountain of life, turning a man from the snares of death. (Proverbs 13:14)

He who ignores discipline comes to poverty and shame, but whoever heeds correction is honored. (Proverbs 13:18)

He who walks with the wise grows wise, but a companion of fools suffers harm. (Proverbs 13:20)

He who listens to a life-giving rebuke will be at home among the wise. (Proverbs 15:31)

Every person in the daily routine begins to look at life through a tube. A mentor can open that constricted world and add depth and beauty with a whole new dimension. An unexamined life, said Socrates, is not worth living.[1] A mentor's wounds are those of a faithful friend. Not everyone has the right to climb into your life and offer rebuke. It must be the mentor who has built a love relationship beforehand. Alfred Whitehead once said, "Apart from blunt truth, our lives sink decadently amid the perfume of hints and suggestions."

Pastor Chuck Swindoll tells the story of a lady who made an appointment with a pastor to talk about joining his church. She said the surgeon who had performed a face lift told her, "My dear, I have done an extraordinary job on your face, as you can see in the mirror. I have charged you a great deal of money and you were happy to pay it. But I want to give you some free advice: Find a group of people who love God and who will love you enough to help you deal with all of the negative emotions inside of you. If you don't, you'll be back in my office in a short time with your face in far worse shape than before."

Mentoring in the Pew

Bruce Larson, who grew up in Chicago and is now pastor of University Presbyterian Church in Seattle, remembers attending a large Gothic Presbyterian church every Sunday. He would wait with anticipation for that awesome moment in the morning service when twelve solemn-faced, frock-coated ushers marched in lock step down the main aisle to receive the brass plates and collect the offering. These men, so serious about their business of serving the Lord in this magnificent house of worship, were leaders of the business and professional community in Chicago.

One of those ushers was a man named Frank Loesch. In Chicago, this imposing man was a legend for he had stood up to the gangster named Al Capone. During the investigations of the Chicago Crime Commission which Frank Loesch had organized, his life was in constant danger. There were threats on the lives of his family and friends, but Mr. Loesch never wavered. His tenacity brought Capone to justice, and Chicago was free of Capone's criminal influence. As he would walk down the aisle, Bruce Larson's father would often have a tear in his eye as he nudged his son and pointed to Loesch.

Who could walk by for you to nudge your son or daughter and say, "There's a person I'd like for a mentor"? I hope that *you* are the person someone is pointing at. The way you treat your spouse, the way you speak to your children, the manner in which you carry out your business — all of this makes you unique, and people are watching with interest and respect.

As Aleksandr Solzhenitsyn completed his lecture before receiving the Nobel Prize for Literature, he made this statement: "One word of truth outweighs the whole world." I'd like to change that to read: "One mentor impacts the whole world." Take, for example, the strategic input of mentor Doug Coe in the life of Chuck Colson at a critical time in the life of the man who formed Prison Fellowship and has helped so many disadvantaged people find Christ as their Savior.

"I have often wondered what would have happened in my Christian life had I not had a mentor like Doug Coe," Chuck said. Doug is part of a movement called "The Fellowship" which works with government officials and peo-

ple in the nation's capital. It is also the group that sponsors the National Prayer Breakfast. Chuck recalls in his
first book, *Born Again*, the divine encroachment upon his
life by God's servant:

> One morning later that week Holly buzzed me on the
> phone. "There's a Mr. Coe here. He wants to see you
> but he won't identify himself. He's probably a reporter;
> those guys are really something." I remembered Tom
> Phillips had said a man named Doug Coe would be
> contacting me. He certainly hadn't wasted any time;
> Tom would barely have gotten my letter.

> Holly, protective as Washington secretaries are trained
> to be, wanted to turn him off. "You'll get yourself into
> something, if I don't." I wanted to tell her that I'd al-
> ready gotten myself "into something."

> Doug Coe moved into my office as if we had known each
> other for years. He greeted me with a wide, friendly smile
> and had one arm around my shoulder before I could
> even invite him to sit down. "This is just great, just great,
> what Tom has told me about you," he said.[2]

Doug continued to minister to Chuck throughout the
months ahead. He prayed with Chuck and regularly
showed him the love of Christ in a way Chuck said he
"never imagined possible."

Doug was also the one who arranged Chuck's visit
with Senator Harold Hughes which is also described in
Born Again:

> My encounter with Senator Harold Hughes was ar-
> ranged for an evening in late September. Harold, I

later learned, had stoutly resisted the idea when Doug
Coe first called him to suggest it.

"There isn't anyone I dislike more than Chuck Colson.
I'm against everything he stands for. You know that,
Doug," he protested.

Before Hughes hung up, Doug gently suggested that
the senator's attitude was hardly Christlike. The next
day Hughes called back and with a weary sigh relented.
"All right, Doug. You set it up."

Fearing that one-on-one confrontation between Harold and myself might be too explosive, Doug decided
to make it a quiet evening with wives, at the home of
the soft-spoken veteran Minnesota Republican congressman, Al Quie. He invited as well a former Demo-
cratic congressman from Texas, Graham Purcell. That
made it two Democrats, two Republicans, and Coe.[3]

The outcome of all this was the formation of links of
friendship whose chain continues to this day. Chuck became part of a small prayer group which consisted of Graham Purcell, the former congressman from Texas, Doug
Coe, Senator Harold Hughes, and Al Quie, then a senior
congressman from Minnesota. These men stood with the
victim of Watergate through all of the travails of prison
and readjustment. It was Congressman Quie who offered
to serve Colson's prison sentence if he could be released
to be home with his family because of the many problems
generated by the sentence.

"Without any question," says Colson, "this group
taught me what a relationship in Christ really means. We
studied our Bibles together, we grew as close as any five
people could be, we poured our hearts out to one an-

other. It was a remarkable and powerful experience which enabled me to grow as a baby Christian. Even after my release from prison, these brothers stayed very close to me and helped me through the early days of the formation of Prison Fellowship. We met regularly until my increasing travel schedule made that impossible.

"As I look back on my Christian life, I realize that my mentoring experiences were absolutely indispensable. Without any question, my experience with Jesus Christ was real, but where it would have led me apart from the patient tutoring and unconditional love of this small group of men is anyone's guess. I've often thought that Prison Fellowship grew out of my obedience to God's call—but that obedience was discipline learned in my relationship with a small group during the first two years of my Christian life."

Intellectual growth, Colson says, "was a second phase of mentoring—and in my view, just as important. Too many young Christians have a dramatic experience, can share their testimony, but that is the end of it. I realized that if God was calling me to a position of leadership, I had to *know* about Him and about the classic doctrines of Christian truth. And so the desire to study and learn, first inspired in me by Dr. Richard Lovelace of Gordon-Conwell Seminary who came to Washington in 1976 and '77 to conduct a class in church history at Fellowship House, was crucial to my own growth and probably to the growth of what has become the largest prison movement in the world. Later I also studied systematically under R.C. Sproul and visited Ligonier Valley Study Center to sit at R.C.'s feet for several years.

"It is because of my personal experiences that we are now emphasizing mentoring in our ministry. We are train-

ing people to work one on one with offenders as they are
released from prison. Our goal is to disciple them just as I
was discipled, to teach them in the ways of the Lord as I
was taught, and to give them the kind of support appara-
tus that I enjoyed."[4]

What kind of mentor impacts the whole world? I
think it would be a person of *vision* who has the ability to
see potential in his protégé, a person not intimidated by
difficulties.

I think it would be a person with *commitment* to go
the distance and make a difference in the life of another.

The mentor would also be a person who gives *priority*
to the kingdom of God and His righteousness.

And finally, I think this kind of mentor would be one
who understands *accountability*, and one whose life is open
to a few trusted confidants and who demands of protégés
the same appraisal. A good mentor believes Matthew
12:36, ". . . men will have to give account on the day of
judgment for every careless word they have spoken. For
by your words you will be acquitted, and by your words
you will be condemned."

Each person gives an account for himself or herself,
not for another. Romans 14:11–12 reminds all that
"'every knee will bow before me; every tongue will confess to God.' So then, each of us will given an account of
himself to God."

Is someone accountable to you so that you can make
them accountable to God? Can you name one or more
people outside your family to whom you have made yourself accountable? Are you aware of the dangers of unac-
countability — dangers such as blind spots, unhealthy relationships, unspoken motives that will never be known
without such a friend? When was the last time you gave

an account for the private areas of your life to someone outside your family? These would include your finances, occupational diligence or lack of it, your attitude at the office, or packing too many hours of work into each day. How about an appraisal of your friendship? Or your struggles with besetting sins?

As a mentor, develop the courage and the right motive to confront. For the good of the protégé and for the good of the Church, "Love must be sincere. Hate what is evil; cling to what is good. Be devoted to one another in brotherly love. Honor one another above yourselves. Never be lacking in zeal, but keep your spiritual fervor, serving the Lord" (Romans 12:9–11).

One word of truth outweighs the world. And one mentor of truth impacts the whole world. That mentor can be you.

Mentoring is a brain to pick, a shoulder to cry on, and a kick in the pants.

John C. Crosby
The Uncommon Individual Foundation

FOUR

MENTORS IN THE HOME

Train a child in the way he should go, and when he is old he will not turn from it.

Proverbs 22:6

Our homes can be the spot of earth supremely blessed — a resort of love, of joy, and of peace, or something quite different when these attributes are absent. How can a person hope to be charitable toward others if he is uncharitable among those of his own kin? And how can a person be effective in mentoring others when those of his or her own household are deprived of the association?

Mentoring Spouses

I have never heard of a person "mentoring" a marriage partner, but I believe it is not only possible but quite necessary. Between a husband and a wife there is a built-in accountability. If there is a breakdown in accountability, a breakdown in the marriage is imminent.

A professional man in his best years was asked, "What is your secret? How do you live in such peace with yourself?" He answered without hesitation: "It is because my wife lives in harmony with herself." And I am certain that, if asked, the wife would answer in the same way about her husband. A husband can accept his masculinity only if his wife accepts her femininity, and of course, it's the other way around as well.

Our Lord touches on this when He commands us to love our neighbor as ourselves (see James 2:8). In this way, He makes self-love in the sense of self-acceptance the yardstick for our attitude toward our neighbor.

Mentors can accept themselves only when they are accepted by others. Married partners can love themselves only if they allow themselves to be loved by others.

My wife, Dorothy, had quietly prayed for my conversion to Christ, and I knew before I even dated her on the campus of Taylor University that I wanted her to be my wife. Interestingly, even though I had asked her for dates during the first year of our college experience together, she would not agree to a date. She had heeded counsel that even though she was attending a Christian college, there could be students who would not be a good influence on her life. I, as an unconverted rascal, was one of those!

Partially through the experience of being turned down by this committed young lady, I was brought under conviction, and through a series of events late in our freshman year, I came to faith in Christ. In no little way this commitment and decision on Dorothy's part was used by the Holy Spirit to bring me into a glorious, life-changing experience with the Savior. Unconsciously, her unswerving commitment became a mentoring experience for me.

Even in the intimacy of marriage bonds, the accountability of mentoring is appropriately applied. The male medical symbol is a circle with an arrow. A man is like an arrow with his interest directed outward. The medical symbol for the female is that of a mirror. The symbol suggests that the wife reflects back and responds to the love which she receives from her husband.

Ingrid Trobisch, a writer of note on this subject both while serving as a missionary with her husband in Africa and while living in Europe, suggests that no man will ever be able to satisfy completely the innermost desires of a woman's heart for love, beauty, and shelteredness.[1] And because of the Fall of Man, it might be said that a woman, too, will always fall short. But together, married couples can look to the One who says, "I have come that they might have life, and have it to the full" (John 10:10), looking forward to the day when we will all be made perfect in Him (see Hebrews 10:14).

Mentors of Children

Psychologist Henry Brandt says that "parenthood is the process of making disciples of your children." Since mentoring is a "subset" of discipling, these suggestions are appropriate as we seek ways to guide our children in the paths they should take.

Before Michelangelo put his chisel to the mighty chunk of granite, he could see in his mind how the statue of David would look when it emerged. Parents, on the other hand, have no control over what that little seven-pound bundle will look like when it appears at the miracle of birth. However, they do have great influence on the development of their child's full potential through mentoring.

My ancestors came from Scandinavia where it was common for a son to take up the trade of his father. Times have changed, of course, and my wife Dorothy and I encouraged our three children to enter whatever vocation they felt the Lord was leading them into.

My job in high school was running a printing press for fifteen cents an hour in my home town of Cleveland, Ohio. Someone snapped a photograph of me as a seventeen-year-old standing at my flatbed press, filling printing orders.

Imagine my surprise and pleasure when our son Don established a successful printing business in Arcadia, California, where he was raised. One day he showed me into his office and pointed at the wall above his desk. There hung an enlarged photograph of me in my coal-bin printing shop with the old flatbed press. How much had my love of printing influenced my son? Quite a lot, apparently, although I had been quite unaware of it.

Not all children have received from their parents the kind of mentoring they need for a rich and full childhood. A U.S. airman stationed in Turkey wrote his testimony for this book project. His story illustrates what just a little help at a critical time might have spared this child:

> As a boy I was very lonely and confused. No one offered to help me out. I tried to make friends in high school but my closest friends were also the other class's "rejects." In college I had a couple of drinking buddies, but since I didn't really like drinking, I spent most of my time either buried in books or basking in loneliness.

My father and his wife thought I was an idiot. I've forgiven them. There was no teacher or other adult who made any great effort to help me out. I made a few idols with no particular reason for doing so but was time and again let down.

Then, after years of being in and out of the church, I found the Lord. But, I hadn't learned my lesson yet. I idolized the pastor and elders at the church I attended until I saw their pompous attitudes tear apart and destroy the congregation. Then, I decided to follow Jesus alone. Since then my entire life has changed. My children have been saved. I married a perfectly wonderful woman. My own attitude has done almost a complete reversal.

I wish a mentor had latched on to me when I was younger and saved me from all those years of hell on earth.

Fathers As Mentors

Before any man can be at his best as a father, he must love his own father. Mine was an expert machinist as well as a lay preacher in the Christian and Missionary Alliance Church. Work was scarce during those Depression years so my mother took housework, and I developed a paper route to help keep our family of six together.

My father never finished high school but did become an accomplished tool and die maker. However, the passion of his life was his lay preaching. He taught me, by example, that a dedicated and committed individual could serve God effectively in the daily marketplace and also have a significant pulpit ministry. Trained as I was in journalism and publishing, I learned from him that I could, as well, have an effective public ministry, for I, too, am a layman who loves to preach. From my dad, years ago, I learned what God could do through a man, even with little education, committed to serving Him. He mentored me, not so much with words of counsel but rather with his committed, exemplary life as husband, father, mechanic, and lay preacher. He never "unsaid" with his life what he said with his lips.

Happy is the daughter who was mentored by her father. Psychotherapist Nancy J. Collins of Rolling Hills Estates, California, is a professional woman whose mentoring father is affirmed as the touchstone of her success. She told me:

"My father was a natural mentor in Alton, Illinois where my twin sister and I grew up. It was easy for me to understand a just and loving Heavenly Father largely because I had seen Him mirrored in the attitudes and actions of Nyal Witham, my dear dad.

"When I would come home from college enraged over society's excesses and unfairness — imagined or real — Dad would quietly hear me out and give credence to my views before offering his balanced perspective in the matter."

Children are made to feel secure by parents who exercise their authority. Young people become afraid when they don't have restrictions. A child may press his parents harder and harder until they finally have to stop him. Some children act that way just to see if the strength they depended on was still there. Children depend on the disciplining of mom and dad to keep them on the right track.

An African proverb states: "Everybody has been young before, but not everybody has been old before." Children who pay attention to the mentoring of an adult are fortunate.

Parents as mentors must function as a unit. Both must make contributions to the raising of the children. If mom's skills are greater in the kitchen, dad can look after the children. Parents can work together to clean the kitchen. Dad can participate in the ritual of getting the children ready for bed. The main point here is: To serve as mentors to their children, both parents need to be involved in *all* aspects of raising children. That way everybody wins.

Parents who agree on major issues are the best mentors to their children. Kindness and respect are twin characteristics of parental mentors who succeed in raising what Zig Ziglar calls "positive kids in a negative world."

Parents who express their love outwardly in front of their children will build security and confidence into their children. This doesn't happen automatically, as illustrated in this poem published in a newspaper more than fifty years ago:

> Two lovers walking down the street.
> She trips, he murmurs, "Careful, Sweet."
> Now wed they tread the selfsame street;
> She trips, he growls, "Pick up your feet."

It was the same street and the same woman, but somehow the irritated husband had forgotten what the lover once knew: how to cherish the woman he loves. What a loss.

One of our three children was a nervous child. Night after miserable night we had to hold our baby to keep it from crying.

"I don't know what else to do," Dorothy confessed. "I've tried everything."

Worn down from loss of sleep, I became angry and impatient. *How could Dorothy be so calm?* I wondered.

The following night brought the same drama. I nudged Dorothy. "You're turn," I grumbled. "The baby's crying again."

My wife staggered up the stairs and soon the baby's cries subsided. Hours later I investigated and found Dorothy slumped in the rocking chair sound asleep, our baby curled in her lap. Dorothy was asleep, her face lined with fatigue and her hair standing up like wood, hay, and stubble, but on her face was a radiant smile. In that moment I understood why she seldom complained. She was suffering for someone she loved.

I greeted her in the kitchen at sunrise with a tray of food and a kiss. "Tonight," I said, "I get to sit up with the baby."

Sometimes a mentor can serve merely by being there.

When James C. Dobson, founder of the popular Focus on the Family enterprise, was a child of three, he slept in a little bed near his parents in a one-room apartment. It was not uncommon during that time for his father to awaken at night and hear a little voice whispering, "Daddy? Daddy?"

James Dobson Sr. would answer quietly, "What, Jimmy?"

Then his son would reply, "Hold my hand."

Father would reach across the darkness and grope for the little hand, finally engulfing it in his. In an instant, the little arm would become limp and the breathing deep and regular. The son only wanted to know that his father was *there*.

Mothers As Mentors

"A woman's love is mighty," says the *Legend of Brittany*, "but a mother's heart is weak, and by its weakness overcomes." Who ran to help you when you fell? Who told lovely stories? Who kissed the place and made it well? Mother, of course. "The bearing and training of a child," said Alfred, Lord Tennyson, "is woman's wisdom."

Women are natural mentors as mothers. They realize the sacred significance of each conception and pregnancy. They treasure each irretrievable moment with their offspring. They know that there will never be another time when they will give birth to their firstborn.

Will your children remember the fun that mom was? Or are you like the woman who suddenly realized one day that she was missing out because she was giving attention only to the physical needs of her children? One mother had regrets about the way she raised her children. A frayed newspaper clipping long out of date contains her plaintive look back.

> I never really looked at my children. When I looked at their mouth, I saw dirt. When I looked at their nose, I saw it running. When I looked at their eyes, I saw them open when I wanted them closed. When I looked at their hair, it needed combing or cutting. I never really looked at the whole face without offering some advice. For twenty years I invited myself into their lives; I put sweaters on them when I was cold; removed blankets from their bed when I was hot; fed them when I was hungry; put them on diets when I was fat; carpooled them when I thought the distance was too far for me to walk; then I told them, they took a lot of *my* time. I never realized that as I dedicated my life to yellow wax buildup and ring around the collar that cleanliness is not next to godliness; *children* are.

Columnist Erma Bombeck puts the mentoring of children into a humorous perspective. She writes:

I always knew that raising kids, if you did it right, might impair you from living a normal life. My tongue was nearly severed by an eight-month-old baby who positioned himself under my chin and then stood up.

Motherhood is definitely not a job for sissies. You must have courage to enter a car with a teenage driver who releases the hood on the expressway, thinking he's turning on the lights.

You must have stamina to drag a preschooler on your leg for two blocks while he is dragging a bubble-gum machine behind him.

You must have firmness to say, "Do not force those car keys up Mommy's nose or Mommy will pass out."

Other mothers have similar stories. One was numb as she checked into a hospital. When she was asked the cause of her dizziness she replied, "I was hit by a truck." She didn't have the heart to tell the admissions nurse that it was a toy dump truck dropped on her from a bunk bed.

Another mother had not seen her son's bedroom for a year and a half. When she pushed open the door and looked in, she lost the sight in her good eye.[2]

A mentoring mother has a vision for each one of her children. She knows that she might have in her arms a judge, a pastor, an inventor, an artist, a musician, an architect, a clear-minded businessman, a statesman.

How could Ada May Day, living on the border of New Mexico and Arizona, ever have thought that her daughter Sandra would become a justice of the Supreme Court? She and her husband had taken Sandra to every capitol dome in the United States. That mother refused to get lost in the morass of everyday living.

Often children are way ahead of mother. They have the perception to think beyond the parent. Children like little Johnny. He said he was drawing a picture of God. "No one has ever seen God at any time," his mother reminded him. "No one knows what he looks like."

"Well," Johnny replied, "they will when I'm through."

Most mothers have one major regret. They are sorry as they look back upon their busy lives that they didn't take time to have more fun. They realize what they missed when they become grandparents and can help the kids log fun times in their memories.

Joseph and Mary didn't grasp the full significance of what was involved in the birth of their firstborn son, but they believed what they were told. Not until Mary stood at the foot of the cross, trembling with agony as she saw Him hanging there naked, with nails in His flesh, His wounds running with blood and saliva, about to die, did she realize the full significance of her mission. It was then that Matthew's prophecy came true and "a sword pierced her heart."

Yes, every mentoring mother who releases her child to fulfill his mission earns the lifetime respect and love of that child.

> If I were hanged on the highest hill
> I know whose love would follow me still,
> Mother o' mine, mother o' mine.
>
> If I were drowned in the deepest sea,
> I know whose tears would come down to me,
> Mother o' mine, mother o' mine.

If I were damned of body and soul,
I know whose prayers would make me whole,
Mother o' mine, O mother o' mine.

Rudyard Kipling
"Mother o' Mine," 1891

Books As Mentors

Some books, wrote Francis Bacon a century ago, are to be tasted, others to be swallowed, and some few to be chewed and digested. Worthy books are like mentors — available as companions and as solitude for refreshment. Thomas Carlyle, in his essays, noted that if time is precious, no book that will not improve by repeated readings deserves to be read at all. I have set a goal to read a book each week, and I can't imagine my life without the companionship of these faithful mentors.

Not long ago, my wife and I were invited to the home of friends to help celebrate the arrival of their firstborn child. As we entered the house, evidence of the newcomer abounded. There were pink ribbons everywhere, pink lemonade, and garlands of flowers that reflected the joy of the proud parents.

Our gift on that occasion was a children's book, a gift that we were afraid might seem odd for such a wee person. But the mother was warmly appreciative.

"Oh," she exclaimed, "we read to our daughter all the time. She loves books."

That baby received a wonderful start in being "mentored" by those friendly companions called books. Good books are honey for a child's heart, but some children will never taste it.

More than twenty-seven million Americans cannot read — not even street signs, medicine labels, or restaurant menus.

Another thirty-three million people read beneath the ninth-grade level ("functionally illiterate"), unable to read and comprehend job instructions, newspaper editorials, or the U.S. Constitution.

The U.S. illiteracy rate is four times higher than the Soviet Union's and five times higher than Cuba's.

Billions of dollars are lost annually in unrealized business productivity due to illiteracy.

An estimated forty-four percent of adults have never read a book in the course of a year.

The average child has seen five thousand hours of TV by the time he graduates from kindergarten.

Upon high school graduation, the average student has watched fifteen thousand hours of TV, compared with twelve thousand hours spent in the classroom.

Average middle-school-age children read books for pleasure for no more than five minutes a day.

The U.S. school dropout rate is twenty-seven percent (Japan's is five percent).

And eighty-one percent of U.S. colleges and universities provide remedial reading courses for freshmen.

Faced with these sobering statistics, parents who read can set a good example for their children. Begin by reading the Bible regularly, and let your children see you reading it. Take time to read to your children, to your spouse, and to friends. Encourage your children to talk about what they're learning and reading. Keep books and magazines handy around the house. Keep your house well lighted so children can read comfortably. Secure a library card for each member of your family. Give books and magazine subscriptions as gifts. Reread a book you loved as a child, then share it with a child. Plan a seasonal reading program. Set family reading goals. Support an annual book fair at your local school. Write book reviews for your church bulletin. And add to this list other creative ideas to encourage children to be mentored by books.

- *Babies and Toddlers.* Choose colorfully illustrated books with simple, short texts or with no words at all.

- *Preschool and Early Elementary.* Children from age four to seven enjoy picture books, especially when humor is combined with fun and with colorful illustrations.

- *Middle Elementary.* Children from age eight to ten, according to reports from the publishing industry, read more books than those in any other age. These children are exhilarated with their newly discovered reading abilities. For the youngest of this group, select "first chapter books," short (under one hundred pages) novels with three- to four-page chapters, usually some line drawings, and larger type with more space between lines than novels for older children.

- *Upper Elementary.* Children in ages ten to twelve often prefer books written for young teens. Help these children to select books that appeal to their widening interests and abilities—books that reflect Christian values. Some books blatantly challenge these values and will confuse your child.

Books serve as mentors not only for children but also for adults, of course. Charles Lamb once said, "I love to lose myself in other men's minds. When I am not walking I am reading; I cannot sit and think. Books think for me."

And while reading the books of other people you can also write some of your own—starting with a journal. Paul

Borthwick, Minister of Missions at Grace Chapel in Lexington, Massachusetts, developed in college the habit of writing in a journal.

> In each spiral notebook "volume," I would write a final page dedicating that edition to someone who had affected me during that time period. In one volume, I made special note of several key figures in my life that year. One had led me in ministry experiences, and another had taught me about preaching. But I had no hesitation in dedicating that volume to the third—a man distinguished by the fact that he had "taught me how to live." His effect on my life was superior because he had exemplified the life he was challenging me to live.[3]

A book is good if it is opened with expectation and closed with profit. The books you choose say much about you. Don't be a one-issue reader. Read widely—even books by authors with whom you disagree. Taste some, chew some, and digest the best. And your children will do the same.

Abraham Lincoln's life illustrates beautifully the value of books as mentors. These storehouses of knowledge caried him through disappointments that would have shattered a weaker man. Among the troubles that visited him were the death of his mother when he was but nine, rejection by his first love, the bankruptcy of his first business venture, defeat the first time he sought public office. . . . Even when he finally made it to Congress, he lasted only one term, being so unpopular that reelection was out of the question. At that point in his life he told a friend, "I will get ready. My time will come."

Remember Abraham Lincoln when you look at your protégé and are tempted to give up. Next to praying "Thy will be done," I can't think of a better expression of faith than, "I will get ready. My time will come."

Mentoring Through Discipline

Some people mistakenly believe that if you discipline your child, he will think you don't love him. Just the opposite is true. Proverbs 13:24 promises: "He who spares the rod hates his son, but he who loves him is careful to discipline him."

The Old Testament uses two Hebrew words to teach correction. The one used in the verse above is *yahsaar*. The word means to chastise, to use the rod, to administer corporal punishment. The earlier a parent disciplines a child, the more hope there is that he will learn respect and enjoy life.

Suzanna Wesley, the mother of eleven children including John and Charles Wesley, believed that the self-willed child must be broken before he reaches the age of two years. He must know by then, she believed, that his will must yield to his parents' word and authority. One of her twenty-one principles for child rearing stated that if ever mentoring needed to be consistent, it is in the mentoring of children. What brought the rod yesterday should bring the rod today.

Proverbs 22:15 again uses *yahsaar*. "Folly is bound up in the heart of a child, but the rod of discipline will drive it far from him." The word *folly* refers not to joking or lightheartedness. It is used here to describe a child who despises discipline, who hates instruction, who mocks at guilt, is quarrelsome and unruly. Children born in sin do not grow out of it without attention to *yahsaar*.

This applies to boys and girls alike. Note what happens to a woman who hasn't received the rod. Proverbs

14:1 declares, "The wise woman builds her house, but
with her own hands the foolish one tears hers down." She
takes up housekeeping with her husband, but then she
gets stars in her eyes and her homelife is ruined.

God wants mentoring parents to create in children a
standard. Parents are to be a living example of what is
right and what is wrong. A child carries away from a good
home a sensitivity gauge. He notices the little red light of
his conscience when it comes on and turns away from
what he had planned to do.

Proverbs 23:13–14 makes a further plea for mentoring
with the rod: "Do not withhold discipline from a child; if
you punish him with the rod, he will not die. Punish him
with the rod and save his soul from death."

Chuck and Cynthia Swindoll have a paddle for each
of their five children. In a moment of good humor, Mrs.
Swindoll glued to the handle on each paddle this prayer:
"God, grant me the courage to change the things that I
can change, the serenity to accept the things I cannot
change, and the wisdom to know the difference. But God,
grant me the courage not to give up on what I think is
right, even though I think it is hopeless."

Pastor Swindoll thinks it's important to use a *rod* as
the Scripture teaches, not the *hand* of the parent. Thus
the child associates the punishment with the paddle and
understands that he is receiving love from the parent.
After he spanked his youngest daughter, Chuck com-
forted her and then left the room. About ten minutes
later she called out, "Daddy."

"What do you want, honey?" he asked.

She pointed to the paddle. "Get that thing out of here."

The second Old Testament word for correction is
yakaag. This word describes God's act of discipline. It

means to convince, to prove, to convict, to rebuke, and frequently it means instruction. "My son, do not despise the Lord's discipline and do not resent his rebuke [*yakaag*]." The reason is: "because the Lord disciplines those he loves, as a father the son he delights in" (Proverbs 3:11–12).

When was the last time you took your child by the arm, pulled him up close, and told him what a delight he is to you? It's not fair to discipline only with the tongue. The rod, sandwiched between instruction and correction, is God's way for parents to mentor their children.

Proverbs 29:15 offers a beautiful balance. It is the same *yakaag* here. This is discipline mixed with delight, instruction, understanding, reasonable spirit, reproof, and anger that is not harsh. "The rod of correction imparts wisdom, but a child left to itself disgraces his mother."

When you discipline your children, never do it in front of any of the other children or when other people are around. Never ask *why* they disobeyed. That only leads to lying or rationalization. Talk instead about *what* was done and remind the child that mother and dad have established rules against that kind of behavior. When they agree to what they have done, it is appropriate to administer the punishment.

Do not let a child scream in rage when he is being spanked. If that happens, he is trying to clear his guilt. You may have to spank a child for his rage until he is crying softly and on his way to repentance. When the discipline has been administered, love and affection are applied. Stay with the child during his moments of crying until a sense of peace returns.

Route 99, the main artery from Los Angeles north through the San Joaquin Valley, runs past Hodel's Family

Buffet in Bakersfield, California. When I see the sign out front, I am reminded of the owner, Bob Hodel, who has established a beautiful relationship with his children, Don and Becky, through mentoring.

One day, when Don was fifteen, he backed a trailer into a pickup truck and dented the side of the truck, while the son of visiting missionaries looked on. A year later, the missionary family returned and in front of Don's parents the son said, "I'll never forget the time you jack-knifed your dad's trailer."

Don was humiliated because he had never told his father how the accident had happened. When the visitors left, Bob and Don went back to hoeing weeds. They worked for about forty-five minutes in silence, when finally Bob looked up and said to his son, "Don, I need to ask you to forgive me. I realize now that I never allowed you to fail and to admit a mistake."

That was the beginning of a relationship that "burned into me a value system I treasure," Don recalls. "It caused me not to expect too much from other people."

Larry Crabb, author of *Inside Out* (Colorado Springs: Navpress, 1988), has concluded from many years of studies in psychology that: "You are a product of your parents, but you can make changes." A mentor is called to help a person make necessary changes for the better.

Bill and Toni Sortor of Harrington Park, New Jersey, recalled the days when their son was a ninth-grade wrestler. He showed up at practice every day, getting sore muscles and bruised ribs. He suited up for each match, but he rarely got to wrestle. His parents wondered why their son was so faithful to his team — working his heart out for the privilege of rolling up the mat at the end of a match.

The parents concluded: "It's all in the coach." In *Daily Guideposts*, 1988, Toni wrote:

> This coach has built a *team*—a team that includes ninth graders and considers them as important as the seniors who do the actual wrestling. A team of back slappers who even clap for one another in practice, win or lose. A team that asks a lot, but gives a lot in return. A kid can be very faithful and work extraordinarily hard for that kind of satisfaction.[4]

It is never too late to recover from a mistake—whether a mistake in dealing with people or in fashioning a work of art. Kuulei Pavao weaves ornamental Polynesian patterns from the slender leaves of the *hala* ("walking tree"). A visitor was especially complimentary toward a work of art, asking if the design were a family secret. Kuulei laughed, explaining that the "traditional" design resulted from a mistake which she saved by inventing a new pattern.

A bird-watching friend tells me there are some things a mentor could learn from the fowl that fly in seemingly perfect formation across the sky. The first lesson is that they take turns at leading; the second is that they honk from behind. For mentor and protégé to reach their destination they must be both leaders and honkers.

Trust is an important word in the mentoring process. In high school, a girl was supposed to end a square dancing routine by reciting "Boop-boop-a-doop," the nonsense phrase of a generation back, then fall backward where another dancer would catch her.

She knew her steps well and performed flawlessly, but the girl could not bring herself to trust her fellow dancer to catch her.

"You've got to trust me," he kept insisting. "I won't let you fall."

At the crucial moment in yet another practice drill, the fellow behind yelled "Trust me!" and as he had promised, he caught the dancer and lifted her to her feet. The dance routine was a hit.

Many times trust has made the difference in a protégé's success or failure. Those of us older in the faith, with more practice in "falling" have come to trust the promises of God and to see our fears fade away.

Lois Walfrid Johnson, author of the Let's-Talk-About-It-Stories for Kids (Navpress), says her husband Roy was a mischievous, curious, fun-loving type—unafraid to try new things. With all of the opportunities for making wrong choices, Roy avoided the trouble that visited his chums. "What made the difference?" his wife asked him one day.

"Because," Roy replied, "I'd think, *My parents trust me. I don't want to let 'em down.*"

As I said earlier, it's never too late to recover from a mistake. But how much better it is when the proper mentoring by parents prevents a child from making a mistake in the first place.

Don't do nothing just because you can't do everything.

Bob Pierce

FIVE

MENTORS IN THE CHURCH

Be shepherds of God's flock that is under your care,
serving as overseers — not because you must, but be-
cause you are willing, as God wants you to be . . .
eager to serve . . . being examples to the flock.

1 Peter 5:2–3

In Tucson, Arizona, one day, Pastor Harold Warner of a church called "The Door" received a card from a young man in his congregation. The card had a Gary Larson cartoon on the front showing a goofy-looking little kid sitting between two rough and tough cowboys in a Western saloon. The youngster had just spilled a glass of milk. One of the cowboys was looking at him and saying, "So . . . you must be the one they call 'The Kid.'" Underneath the cartoon Pastor Warner's parishioner had written, "Yes, and I want to be discipled." He added elsewhere on the card more formally: "I

69

would like to express my desire to be discipled, counselled and formed by you and the men of your likemindedness."

"My young friend was expressing a genuine need," said Pastor Warner. "He wanted more than just a handbook or an instruction manual. He wanted a mentor, someone who had been where he wanted to go."

Pastor Warner's mentor, the Rev. Wayman Mitchell in Prescott, Arizona, used to tell him: "People are not very good at taking orders but they are great at imitating." That is an important part of the mentoring process described in this chapter.

The poet Ralph Waldo Emerson, with a grand sweep of his eloquent pen, wrapped up the theme of this book with one well-crafted sentence: "Our chief want in life is somebody who shall make us do what we can."[1] This is a beautiful way of underscoring both the joy and responsibility of mature members of a congregation, beginning with the pastor, in serving as mentors to the flock of God.

The Pastor Mentor

Nobody knows better than pastors the critical shortage of leaders in the Church today and the worldly encroachments into the existing leadership. Forward-looking pastors desire to add the useful third dimension of mentoring to a congregation's evangelistic and worship programs. It is long overdue. The church is probably seeing as many decisions for Christ today as it ever has in its history, but it has too often allowed the world to be the agent of change in the lives of its members rather than taking its cues from the Great Shepherd represented by the pastor.

The ideal mentor/pastor must be born again, filled with the Holy Spirit, and skilled in what Professor Allan

Coppedge calls three essential principles: life-to-life transference, spiritual disciplines, and accountability.[2]

"Life transference," in the view of Dr. Coppedge, occurs when a pastor shares wisdom, knowledge, experience, and maturity with a parishioner in unstructured situations. Most people learn more effectively when they hear a concept and then see it demonstrated in real-life situations. The principle of life transference as modeled by Jesus' relationship to the Twelve is discussed in the final chapter of this book.

The phrase "spiritual disciplines" of a mentor refers to the discipline of paying the price for developing a warm and strong relationship with God. This includes the discipline of time with His Word, of Scripture memory, of fellowship with other believers, of giving generously, of prayer, of fasting, and of worship.

"Accountability" is also crucial to the mentoring process as noted in chapter three. The Twelve were accountable to Jesus; the disciples were also accountable to each other as they went out two by two. Being accountable means that members of the body of Christ care enough for one another to hold each other responsible for developing a relationship with God, growing in His likeness, and accomplishing His work in the world.

Accountability in the church family can be judgmental, strict, and impersonal as well as warmly supportive and challenging. The object is to hold people accountable so that they may develop to their full potential.

Richard C. Halverson, chaplain of the U.S. Senate and a man with whom I worked closely for many years, describes as his mentor the man who led him to Christ in March of 1934 — David Cowie. Halverson, at twenty years of age, loved his pastor so much that he came close to wearing out his welcome in the pastor's study at the Vermont Avenue Presbyterian Church in Los Angeles.

"My pastor practiced tough love," Halverson recalls, "daring to confront my weakness, failure, and sin—but always in the spirit of God's forgiveness and love.

"I was in his office so much that he finally had to ask me not to come so that he could get other things done. 'Please,' I begged, 'just let me sit with you in your office. I won't say a word.' Imagine! A kid twenty years of age. My pastor insisted that I spend every summer during college and seminary days working at the church under his supervision. I learned more from my pastor than I did from three years in a theological seminary. He was a genius in administration, had a deep love for the Word of God, and was committed to expository preaching."[3]

What qualifies a pastor to become a mentor? George Fraser, executive vice president of the Titus Task Force in Bakersfield, California and a former troubleshooter for the Federal Government before obeying a call from "up higher," sees in the opening verses of the First Epistle of John the ideal description of a pastor/mentor:

". . . which we have *heard*."

This describes verbal instruction, admonition, and comfort in a teaching situation as part of the training of a mentor.

". . . which we have *seen* with our eyes."

This implies that the mentor had a mutual experience with someone that is worth sharing. It's one thing to hear, but an important added dimension to be able to see the implications of what has been heard.

". . . which we have *looked at*."

To see is to observe but to look at is to analyze, to move into a deeper level of discernment about what is going on.

". . . and [which] our hands have *touched*."

This describes the experience of being with someone and being involved in circumstances with active, intentional risk. I may hear it, see it, look at it . . . but only when I reach out and *touch* this person do we move into a level where we finally come to the meaning of what mentoring is all about.

George Fraser says his mentors in the faith have been those who:

1. built a relationship with me, showing interest in me and sharing their personal lives with me.

2. were bold, yet caring, in admonishing me and instructing me in appropriate behavior.

3. made certain their teaching was "show and tell," not merely "tell."

4. offered teaching that has been a constant guide and encouragement.

5. stood by me in my sufferings through ignorance and stupidity for righteous causes.

6. supported me in times of risk when safety would have been compromised.

Mentoring is much more expansive than simply teaching and/or training. It is investing time and prayer. It is building relationships and investing emotionally in the transfer of values and skills and attitudes. Discipling talks about discipline, while mentoring talks about a relationship. Mentoring can't happen outside the context of relationship. No one is in a better position to carry this out than the shepherd.

Dr. Paul S. Rees, a distinguished pastor and an associate of mine for more than a quarter of a century, has become a pastor to pastors in remote parts of the world through conferences established especially for the training of indigenous workers. But even this eloquent preacher was helped at the start of his career by a good mentor. This is how Dr. Rees tells it:

> He was twenty years my senior, and when you are only twenty-three the difference seems prodigious. Add to that the fact that he had already won his spurs as a Methodist minister in such fields as pastoral care, high-level evangelism, and now was being recognized in higher Christian education.
>
> Capture the scene. The twenty-three-year-old beginner is assigned to preach at an interdenominational service in which *he* — of the raven-black hair, he of the piercing dark eyes, he of the marvelously controlled resonant voice — will be a listener. As I had to leave immediately after the meeting for a distant appointment, there was no time for him to take me aside and evaluate the sermon. I had reason to believe that he would be as perceptive about its theology as he was about its spiritual quality. What I did not know was that his fine-tuned empathy would reach out to the *manner* of the sermon's delivery, the *mechanics* of it, if you can tolerate so crass a way of describing it.
>
> When, therefore, I received from him a long letter, most of which dealt with the sermon he had heard me preach, I was trembly but trusting.
>
> In a disarming, fatherly way he suggested that my voice-use needed discipline. There was no alternation of loudness and softness that would have improved the

quality of communication. Specifically, he noted that I used the same vocal intensity in giving an illustration as was used in scoring an important climax. "Your voice needs resting," he wrote, "and story-telling is one way to rest it." That lesson alone proved to be a life-long boon.

That letter, as I can now gratefully testify, proved to be the beginning of a long friendship in which, both by example and by conversation, he became my tactful, faithful advisor and model.[4]

Lay Mentoring

You can attend church until you are a hundred and be terribly theoretical. But when you have a mentor who meets with you and works with you and spends time in friendship, reproof, and mutual projects, the truths of the Bible comes to life in shoeleather.

The mentoring process is wide open, of course, for the laity. It is not for the faint of heart. Sometimes a mentor will be called upon to give a protégé straight talk about an improper attitude, about a wrong choice, about a problem unresolved. I can think of no better example of this than an incident which happened at the close of a year-long training program sponsored by Interns for Christ in Southern California.

A candidate (we'll call him John) enrolled for the internship program with a view to joining Overseas Crusades to work in South America. John was tall, good-looking, talented as a speaker, skillful in learning Spanish, and clever with his guitar.

The time came for Norm Cook of Overseas Crusades to fly in for the final interview and to hear the verdict of the leaders of Interns for Christ on John's fitness for service. The executive director said little as he rode along to the airport in John's car to meet Norm Cook. This was to be his protégé's big moment, and yet he felt that something wasn't right. "Well," said John as he parked his car and switched off the engine, "are you going to tell Norm Cook I'm ready for the assignment?"

The director was silent for a long moment. Then he turned to him and said quietly, "I'm going to tell Norm Cook that you're a phony."

John looked at him as though he had been struck with a fist. Then he grew angry and defensive as he thought about the implications of that statement for his family, his supporters, and his mission board. John gripped the steering wheel and laid his head against it. Overhead, Norm Cook's plane was circling and would soon land. John's life-long dreams had been shattered.

"Why do I think you're a phony?" the director asked.

"Because," John whispered, "I am. I accepted Christ as my Savior at sixteen and it's been a game ever since. I got straight A's in school and I cheated on everything and . . . yeah, you're right. I am a phony."

The director prayed silently, searching for the right verse of Scripture to encourage his young friend. He gripped the arm of his protégé and said, "God will not test you beyond what you can bear."

Norm Cook met the two men on schedule in a corridor of the airport terminal and exchanged greetings. When Norm turned to the director and asked, "Well, what's the verdict?" he didn't have to wait long for the answer. John himself laid out his own charade and asked for another chance. Another year of training and grooming was granted the young missionary candidate, and

today he is faithfully serving Christ effectively in the bar-
rios of Colombia.

John's mentor was able to see both his strengths and
his weaknesses. The mentor was able also to have a clear
vision of what his protégé could and could not do, because to take a person beyond what he can do is to teach
him nothing but failure. A mentor must be sure of his
relationship with the Lord, otherwise he cannot endure a
protégé's rejection, anger, and frustration as he is being
stretched. And if a mentor is not stretching his protégé,
he does not have a mentoring relationship.

One of the most fascinating stories of lay mentoring is
contained in a letter just received from my friend Tony
Campolo. Challenged by the theme of this book, he
reached back in his memory and recollected days in his
native Philadelphia when a lay mentor took the time to
make an impact on his life for Christ and His Kingdom.

When Tony was in high school, a friend of his invited
him to attend a Bible study that met on Saturday eve-
nings. The idea of a bunch of city kids getting together to
study the Bible on a Saturday night seemed strange, but
his friend was such a good guy that Tony couldn't turn
him down.

Approximately forty high school kids squeezed into
the living room and dining room of a small row house in
West Philadelphia for a meeting led by an accountant
named Tom Roop. They had given the group the unlikely
name of "Bible Buzzards," and their enthusiasm matched
that of their teacher.

Tom Roop was anything but impressive-looking. He
was a very serious man with a neatly trimmed, thin mous-
tache. After some singing, he had the group open their

Bibles, and on that first night of Tony's appearance, he focused on Paul's letter to the Philippians.

"Tom was an excellent Bible teacher," Tony recalls, "but there was more to him than that. He had time for us and he certainly had a lot of time for me."

Tony Campolo continued to attend those Saturday night gatherings. Tom made it clear that he wanted to be his friend.

"I was always welcomed to his home," Tony recalls. "Some of my close buddies and I took advantage of his hospitality. Over the next three years I spent a great deal of time with Tom, sitting around with him in his living room, going with him on speaking engagements, and attending the Bible clubs that gave him an opportunity to share his views on nearly every subject possible. There wasn't anything that went on in my life that I did not run by him. He very much became my spiritual father and mentor."

That Bible study group in the accountant's house was a prime factor in molding Tony Campolo into the dynamic speaker and writer he is today. Added to the Saturday night meetings were youth retreats, special evangelistic rallies, and even a week-long summer Bible conference sponsored by the club for hundreds of kids in the inner city.

In each of those activities, Tom sat back and let the young guys who were under his supervision do the planning and the leading. He was never the up-front song leader. He was never the one who laid the plans, but he was always there to provide counsel and direction and critiquing. He let his "Bible Buzzards" be the leaders, as only a secure mentor could. He helped them to evaluate what they were doing as only a Biblically astute man could.

"Out of that group of forty young people," writes Tony, "came more than a dozen preachers, two professors of theology who teach at seminaries, and more than a half-dozen missionaries.

"Tom Roop was the best example I know of what a man who is willing to invest his time in mentoring young people can accomplish for the kingdom of God."

Mentoring by Setting an Example

The Apostle Paul wrote to the Roman believers, "But God demonstrates his own love for us in this: While we were still sinners, Christ died for us" (Romans 5:8). The example that Jesus set showed us love that is given without reciprocation. We were helpless, but He gave Himself; we had nothing to offer Him.

Amy Carmichael, founder of the Donhavur Fellowship in India, exhorts believers to give without reciprocation in their commitment to follow Christ:

> Hast thou no scar?
> No hidden scar on foot, or side, or hand?
> I hear thee sung as mighty in the land,
> I hear them hail thy bright ascendant star:
> Hast thou no scar?
>
> Hast thou no scar?
> Yet, I was wounded by the archers, spent,
> Leaned against the tree to die, and rent
> By ravening beasts that compassed me, I swooned:
> Hast thou no wound?
>
> No wound? No scar?
> Yes, as the master shall the servant be,
> And pierced are the feet that follow Me;

> But thine are whole. Can he have followed far
> Who has no wound? No scar?[5]

Bernie May, Director of Wycliffe Bible Translators, succeeded a man who had founded the organization in 1934. Few men in this century affected the cause of missions by example as much as Cameron Townsend. When I met "Uncle Cam," he was already a legend. And to Bernie, an aviator with Wycliffe's flying arm, the Jungle Aviation and Radio Service, he was truly a mentor.

In thinking back on his relationships with "Uncle Cam" Bernie writes:

Uncle Cam was not a teacher, yet I learned nearly all I know about missions, about cross-cultural involvement, about management and sales, and about leadership from him. In looking back I now realize what I learned was caught, not taught. He never sat me down and said, "Now Bernie, pay close attention to what I'm about to say." He never told me what to do. Instead, he was the kind of man who said, "Follow me." And I did.

Sometimes from afar. At other times by his side.

Those of us who watched him work did not realize what had taken place until we came up against certain circumstances. Then there would be a flashback and we would say, "Oh, that's the way Uncle Cam would have done it."

He seldom directed. Instead, he was always giving suggestions. His favorite approach to a situation was to say, "I wonder if it wouldn't be a good idea if we would . . ." And those of us who worked closest to him realized that was a direct command. Yet his purpose was always to make us feel that it was our idea, not his.

Several years after I moved to Peru I was elected chairman of the Executive Committee — which was the equivalent of being senior deacon in a church. Uncle Cam, who was general director of Wycliffe worldwide, came to me one hot, muggy afternoon. I had just come in from a long jungle flight in a single-engine float plane. I had flown out the night before, landed on the Maranon River and gotten up early the next morning to load two translators and their baby into the plane. They had an Indian language helper with them — plus a small cage with two monkeys and assorted baggage. It was a three-hour flight back and Uncle Cam was waiting for me when I landed.

"Bernie," he began, "what do you think about inviting the Minister of Education out to the center for a reception?"

"It sounds like a grand idea to me," I said. "We need to have more contact with the government officials."

The following day I was attending a meeting of the Executive Committee when I heard Uncle Cam say, "Bernie thinks we ought to invite the Minister of Education to come out from Lima to attend an anniversary reception at the center. I agree with him."

Everyone else agreed too — and suddenly I was in the middle of all the details.

Uncle Cam was constantly giving credit to others — and to God. "Isn't it wonderful," he told a group of us one time, "how God has laid it on the heart of the President of Mexico to open the doors to enlarged ministry in the nation." We all agreed. It wasn't until much later that I learned that God had a lot of help from Uncle Cam who had spent days sitting in the waiting room outside *El Presidente's* office until the president finally capitulated and gave him an audience.

When I think of the primary thing I learned from him it was this: Work real hard—and expect a miracle. Or, as another Wycliffe leader once put it: We do our best; God does the rest.[6]

It's no accident that Gene Getz became the youngest professor ever to teach at Moody Bible Institute (MBI) in Chicago. Gene went to MBI from a religious sect called the Apostolic Christian Churches of America in the farm area one hundred miles south of Chicago where he grew up. Though the plain group had espoused confusing doctrines, Gene's mentor Dr. Harold Garner at MBI became the one to help the young man "rightly divide the Word of Truth" and become an effective Christian teacher, writer, and administrator. Gene Getz is the founder of Fellowship Bible Church in Dallas, Texas, which now has expanded to some seventeen churches in the metroplex and some one hundred and fifty churches throughout the United States. He is the author of seven study books, five devotional books, and many scripts for audiovisual materials for churches.

"It was Dr. Garner's encouragement when he believed in me even though I didn't believe in myself," says Dr. Getz. "He encouraged me to write when I didn't think I could; he wanted me to go on for further education when I didn't think I could ever do it."[7]

Gene went on to get his doctorate at New York University and later joined the faculty at Dallas Theological Seminary in Texas.

In his wallet Gene carried for many years this little piece of prose given to him by his mentor:

> O the comfort, the inexpressible comfort,
>   of feeling safe with a person;
>   having neither to weigh thoughts,
>   nor measure words,
>   but to pour them all out, just as it is,
>   chaff and grain together,
>   knowing that a faithful hand
>   will take and sift them,
>   keeping what is worth keeping, and then,
>   with a breath of kindness,
>   blow the rest away.

Ken Wendling, founder of LIFE Ministries with evangelism outreach through language teaching in Japan and mainland China, began his work after God called him out of an enterprising business in southern California. Among the three men Ken chose to list as his mentors was the curious name of Gen Takahashi. Formerly a trade representative and an executive with Marubene Corporation in Tokyo, this diminutive man became an employee of LIFE Ministries after his retirement.

Ken recalls with amusement:

When I first met him, I mistook him for an employee of Marubene Corporation. But as the years have rolled by, Gen Takahashi has become a much-trusted mentor. He established a caring presence through his availability. Often the informal agendas which we would frequently discuss gave us an opportunity not only to solve the immediate difficulty or challenge or management decision, but also to establish certain values which could only be transmitted with the passing of time.

One important lesson Ken learned from this layman was that important decisions and values require time. They often result in error if they are needlessly hurried.

> The difference between the way a Japanese and an American makes a decision is a good example. In the case of an American, the decisions often can be made quickly and then extensive discussions occur to create a consensus to move the enterprise toward its objective. In Japan, the process is just the opposite (a management value I learned from Mr. Takahashi): Build the consensus carefully, develop the relationships, create an understanding for the issue at hand, then the decision will belong corporately to the enterprise and the group can move more expeditiously towards its objective. While the 'first end' activity may appear to be nonactivist, the goal is reached more efficiently.[8]

Mentoring by Serving

Moses and David tended sheep; Stephen served tables; and followers of Jesus Christ down through the centuries have been model servants toward others in the building of the kingdom.

Jesus said, "If you are willing to be last, then you will be first. If you're willing to do the small things, then I will make you ruler over many things."

Mentoring by serving embraces a Biblical paradox: we gain by losing and become great by becoming small. To evade the Cross is to cut ourselves off from the possibility of true spiritual mentoring—the kind our nation needs more than ever.

At World Vision, young people like Hector Jolija and John Yale have become mentors in a difficult, war-torn, poverty-stricken country where the human rewards are few. They often fall ill, sometimes fear for their lives and the lives of their families, and are overwhelmed by the needs around them. They are in Mozambique because they are obedient. They know that to love Christ is to love the people for whom He died, regardless of the risks. C.S. Lewis wrote of the risks involved in mentoring others:

> Love anything, and your heart will certainly be wrung, possibly be broken. If you want to make sure of keeping it intact, you must give your heart to no one, not even an animal. Wrap it carefully round with hobbies and little luxuries; avoid all entanglements; lock it up safe in a casket or coffin of your selfishness. But in that casket—safe, dark, motionless, airless—it will change. It will not be broken; it will become unbreakable, impenetrable, irredeemable. . . . The only place outside heaven where you can be perfectly safe from all the dangers and perturbations of love is hell.[9]

Discipleship Journal, published by The Navigators in Colorado Springs, asked six prominent Christians why the nation had a shortage of leaders.[10] I include their answers here because leadership, by definition, is linked with mentoring.

- Dr. Richard C. Halverson, U.S. Senate chaplain, summed up the role of a leader (and of a mentor as well) with Matthew 5:13–14: "You are the salt of the earth. . . . You are the light of the world" and cautions that all the "skills" and "how-to's" taught in the evangelical community have not had much moral impact on our society. "The Church does not need more 'leadership training,'" he says. "What we need is 'righteousness training.'"

- Elisabeth Elliot Gren, author and speaker, believes that the Church will be more effective in raising up leaders when we begin to teach and exemplify servanthood and live by the principle of obedience.

- Beverly LaHaye, founder and director of Concerned Women of America, notes that leadership is hampered by fear. "The principle that has motivated me more than any other—especially when I'm fearful about taking a step in a leadership role—is to tell myself over and over, 'God is directing my steps. I can do it!'"

- Rebecca Manley Pippert, National Consultant on Evangelism for InterVarsity Christian Fellowship, feels that the problem is not that there are too few qualified leaders but that there is too little opportunity for thousands of capable Christian women to use their leadership abilities in the Church. "We have vastly overemphasized leadership skills at the expense of character," she says.

- Gordon Loux, former president and chief executive officer of Prison Fellowship Ministries, believes that one reason for the shortage of leadership throughout the Christian community is that too many Christian leaders have been strong, independent types.

- Lorne Sanny, chairman of The Navigators' U.S. board of directors and former president of the organization, believes that one reason leaders are scarce is that a true leader must also become a manager—and it's hard to do both.

The theme verse for the symposium was 1 Corinthians 4:1, "So then, men ought to regard us as servants of Christ and as those entrusted with the secret things of God."

A mentor is not primarily a servant of people, but of Christ. Unless we get that clear, we're always going to be on pins and needles, because we can't please everybody.

Mentoring by Empathizing

A journalist who followed Bob Pierce, founder of World Vision, through Asia once commented: "To understand how much a person is suffering look not at the cripple or the beggar or the orphan but at Bob Pierce's face as he seeks to help them."

Larry Ward, who worked with Bob Pierce in World Vision from 1957 to 1970 before founding Food for the Hungry, recalls choice phrases which show the depth of his empathy for a lost and dying world. Here are excerpts from Larry's letter on his mentor:

"Don't tell me it can't be done until you have spent at least four hours trying."

I don't know how many times I heard Bob Pierce say this in the twelve or so years of our close association. Nor do I know exactly what magic he saw in the "four hours" stipulation. But I heard it often — and I learned each time.

Illustration: The sad-faced Japanese film crew stood there, shaking their heads in the massive Festival Hall in Osaka, Japan. "We know not enough light, Dr. Pierce. But no way get enough lights here in Osaka. Maybe in Tokyo — but not in Osaka."

Bob Pierce's booming voice echoed off the walls of Festival Hall. "Don't tell me that until you have spent at least four hours trying," he roared.

Four hours later they came in, one by one, each one dragging probably enough equipment to have lit the entire place just by itself.

"Anything worth doing is worth doing right."

Bob Pierce might be late for the banquet at which he was the featured speaker or for his meeting with the high official. I confess I never felt comfortable about that aspect. But—he was always ready. His suit was pressed; his shoes were shined. He may have just flown in from another country, but he was relaxed and ready . . . and somehow able to devote his full attention to the matter at hand and to the people with whom he was dealing.

The most important thing in succeeding is just plain lasting.

This was a guiding principle for my mentor, Bob Pierce, and he pounded this point home again and again. Often it was when he was confessing his own deep and prayerful desire that, in the words of Scripture, "His end might be greater than his beginning."

"Anybody can do a good job with about ninety-five percent effort. It's that last five percent of effort that makes a great job."

I don't know where Bob found the magic in the five percent any more than in the four hours referred to in his other statement. But time and again, not only from his words but from his example, I saw what an overriding principle this was for him.

"Do it, Buddy. Don't just say it. Do it."

This was my mentor's passion . . . and I think he communicated it to me. And this great driving motivation of his, for which I could supply a thousand illustrations, led to his attitude and tone of near-contempt when he saw someone who was a talker and not a doer.

"And do it now."

To Bob Pierce, the important thing was not only to do something—to follow through on promises—but always to do something "now." When he was in the midst of need, one thing he made sure of was that he did something—whatever it was—while he was there, before he left.

Pastor Bill Hybels writes:

Empathy [or compassion] does not come naturally to us hardhearted people. We have to slow down and make a determined effort to put ourselves in other people's shoes. We need to ask ourselves how it would feel to be in their situations.[11]

Hybel adds this bit of advice for the mentor who serves by empathizing:

How would it feel to be handicapped, unable to stand up, walk, dress yourself, drive or even find a good seat in church because there is no room for your wheelchair?

How would it feel to be unemployed, to have a mortgage and car payments you cannot make and to have children you cannot provide for?

How would it feel to be Black in a White community that is not particularly sensitive to minorities?

How would it feel to be divorced, to be widowed, to lose a child or parent?

How would it feel to have cancer, multiple sclerosis, Alzheimer's disease or AIDS?[12]

Joni Eareckson Tada knows what disability is like. Joni still considers Steve Estes to be her spiritual mentor. He was a sixteen-year-old boy at the time they met, but he had a great love for God's Word and a desire to help Joni out of her depression following her diving accident in Maryland more than twenty years ago.

"There are still times," she says, "when I wonder to myself, 'How would Steve handle this?' So yes, my friend

Steve is still a mentor to me (with my husband's approval and appreciation)."

When King David went to the cave of Adullam, the Bible says that "all those who were in distress or in debt or discontented gathered around him, and he became their leader [mentor]" (1 Samuel 22:2). These four hundred men saw in David a leader, a man of God. David was able to inspire them to undertake a holy enterprise. As a result, the kingdom was established under David's rule.

2 Samuel 21:20–22 tells the story of huge men descended from Goliath who fell "at the hands of David *and* his men." The stirring truth is that what David was, these men became. That's *mentoring*.

Neighborhood Mentoring

In the sixties, a group of concerned lay Christians formed Mariners Church in Newport Beach, California. It was a congregation independent of denominational ties and innovative in its approach to ministry throughout the beach cities.

Several years ago Hudd Saffell, one of the original board members, saw a need in the church for older couples to serve as mentors to younger couples in their neighborhoods. He created a program called "GenSpan" and formalized its goals which he presented to all who would accept the challenge and participate by opening their homes on week nights. The program had a three-fold objective:

1. To experiment with the concept that marriage and family experience can be transferred from older couples to younger couples in an effective

and profitable manner. (see Deuteronomy 6:1–9; Judges 2:8–12; Psalm 37:23–25)

2. To discover all available information from Scripture designed to promote loving relationships and to develop appropriate application. (see 2 Timothy 3:16, 17)

3. To encourage and care for one another and thereby create an intimate family; to mature in Christ together. (see Hebrews 10:24–25)

Prospective leaders were encouraged to write out an interpretation of the responsibilities of the husband and the wife found in Ephesians 5:22–33 and then attend an opening night in the home of Hudd and his wife Joanne in Emerald Bay nearby.

Hudd prepared a cursory outline for prospective Gen-Span leaders which read as follows:

December 8, 1986

As believers in Christ, our primary reason for any effort is to advance the cause of the Gospel, help our brothers and sisters to mature in the faith, and strengthen our own faith in God. With this in mind, along with the three-fold objective of GenSpan, one can prepare a varied menu of study and yet accomplish the objectives and goals.

Some of the menu items we employed are listed below; they may prove helpful to you in your leadership:

Getting acquainted with one another is a very important phase of the work. We have used such activities as going to a movie; arranging a picnic; enjoying a potluck supper; dinner on the beach, etc. A creative approach to getting acquainted offers extra fun and pleasure. So, salt the program with these or similar activities for a faster warm-up to a "family" group.

There have been many opportunities to counsel or advise our "family" members and these have led to better understanding and closer relationships. We all have needs and when help is required it is comforting to discuss our problems with an older person, unrelated.

We have used some well-known Bible stories for discussion topics and found them to be most profitable learning:

- Hannah's Honor . . . A Lesson in Trust and Obedience, 1 Samuel 1:1–2:11; 2:20–21; 3:19–21. [Assignment sheets were attached]

- Abigail . . . A Woman with Character, 1 Samuel 25:1–42.

- Eli's Disgrace . . . Let's Talk About Raising Kids! 1 Samuel 2:12–17; 22–25; 27–29; 30–32; 33–36; 4:10–22.

- David and Bathsheba . . . .A Terrible Plot, 2 Samuel 11:1–12:25; 1 Kings 1:11–31; Psalm 51.

Many lessons and close relationships grew out of the GenSpan experiment both for older couples who led the sessions and for the younger ones who were the learners. Meeting on a midweek evening, the group:

- Formed close relationships with active, young couples which became lasting associations.

- Learned, firsthand, the problems which the younger generation faces, which differ from those encountered a generation earlier.

- Developed a curriculum which would assist others to lead such a group.

- Discovered new truth from the Scriptures regarding marriage and marriage relationships.

- Observed needs of others and prayed for answers and solutions.

- Gained great satisfaction by recognizing that objectives were honestly met and were beyond expectations.

- Maintained a sense of "family" with all the participants and a joy in watching each couple grow in the Lord.

The GenSpan sessions answered many and varied questions from the younger couples. One practical matter involved a brother's dilemma with regard to a sister. Her car was being repossessed by the bank, and he was worried about lending his sister any more money. He had done it before, and it always led to hard feelings. The problem was solved when the GenSpan leader suggested that his sister ask the bank to renew the loan and offer smaller payments so the sister could keep the car.

Another husband found guidance through GenSpan in dealing with a troublesome employer.

Still another asked GenSpan leader Hudd Saffell, who had been a builder, to walk through a new house they wanted to purchase to see if it was sound. The retired builder inspected the structure carefully, noted improprieties and poor workmanship, showed the couple how to have them solved, and helped them to move into their dream home with satisfaction.

"In every act of mentoring," said Saffell, "we aren't helping anyone if we are conveying to them something that isn't scriptural, something distorted, or something off the top of our heads. A scriptural mentor must be on track with the Word of God."

The Apostle Paul exhorted older men to work with younger men and older women to work with younger women. What church do you know of that carries out this Biblical plan—having older Christians work with younger ones? Yet I am confident that there are younger Christians in most churches who are yearning for faithful input from wise, sweet people in the faith who have learned through the hard knocks of experience.

My wife and I saw firsthand the value of neighborhood mentoring soon after we moved to southern California. One day when Dorothy was shopping for our Thanksgiving dinner, she reached for a can of cranberry sauce just as another woman had spotted it. Both of their hands landed on the can at precisely the same moment, and both women insisted the other take it. The manager had another in the store room, which would have ended the matter except that God had something in mind for Bette Vessey, her husband Ned, and their children.

"Our family needed Jesus our Savior," said Bette Vessey later, "and this was God's way of bringing us into His Kingdom. I used to see Dorothy out pulling weeds, little realizing that as she worked she was praying for the Vesseys."

Ned and Bette accepted an invitation to attend a meeting of the Laymen's Leadership Fellowship and eventually joined a prayer group in the neighborhood.

Bette wrote:

The Engstroms introduced us to leading Christians,
and drew us into a loving circle of friends. They helped
us buy helpful Christian books. On Saturdays when I
would see Ted cleaning his garage, I would stop and
pin him against the garage door with questions about
God's Word and about the books I was reading. If he
disapproved of some far-out books I had bought, he
would throw them away.[13]

Out of this association came a friendship with Herb
and Betty Hawkins who also lived in the neighborhood and
salvation for both the couple and their children. Ned Vessey is now with the Lord, but Bette still points back to the
neighborhood mentoring as the means of grace that
brought them salvation, joy unspeakable, and eternal hope.

My children, grandchildren, and two great grandchildren belong to Jesus because a vivacious and lovely
lady and I met at Ralph's supermarket—both reaching
for the only can of cranberries left on the shelf. Our
hands met and the spark of Jesus flowed through them
to eventually flow to many others and even to different
generations. I'm sure that Ted and Dorothy Engstrom
were sent from Wheaton in 1963 just for *me*.[14]

Our neighbors, all of them, were of greater blessing to
us, I'm sure, than we were to them. But the lesson remains: Each Christian has the wonderful privilege of helping to build the Church beginning with mentoring in his
own backyard.

How to Spot a Toxic Mentor

1. The Avoider

"Of course we'll get together, but I'm too busy today."

Initial enthusiasm but later inaccessibility. Not available when the need is greatest. Cannot get close emotionally. Unintentionally forgets to share organizational information.

2. The Dumper

"A protégé? I'd love a dedicated assistant!"

Opposite to the Avoider, is delighted to give you opportunities, assignments, extra work, more responsibility . . . but, inadequate guidance; you are abandoned.

3. The Criticizer

"Let me take this opportunity to show you why that's not the right way to do it."

Believes mentoring is a license to point out mistakes. Gives you responsibility, maybe too much too soon, and then criticizes you for inexperience and poor performance. Unconsciously keeps you subordinate.

4. The User

"My wife doesn't understand me." "You're not breaking up anything; we were already pretty far apart."

You are the mentor's spy in the ranks. You run up the flags. You are a convenient, pleasant companion, backboard, or source of ideas.

5. *The Black Halo*

"You have the perfect mentor—only anyone associated with that person becomes poison in the company."

The mentor teaches you all there is to know—only policy changes and that way of operating is out of favor.

6. *The Queen Bee*

"I made it in a much tougher time by myself. You can, too."

Doesn't believe that you should show that you need help. The Attrition Theory: "I made it by hard work / brains / luck, but they made it by knowing someone!"

Richard H. Tyre
The Uncommon Individual Foundation

VOCATIONAL MENTORS

Never be lacking in zeal, but keep your spiritual fervor, serving the Lord.

Romans 12:11

M entors in the world of business, the arts, education, finance, politics, military, and the trades play an important role in the success of every vocational endeavor. Organizations with reputations for developing leaders attract the best leaders. Even when economic pressures are keen, the mentoring process must not be neglected by those charged with the responsibilities of corporate management.

I appreciate the perceptive words of my friend Dick Halverson, who wrote in the preface of his book *Perspective:*

> I dedicate my book to faithful Christian laymen who, with silent heroism under relentless secular pressure, fight the economic battle as stewards of the living God.[1]

Studies show that mentoring on both informal and formal levels can increase job satisfaction, job performance, and employee loyalty and result also in a decrease in turnover. In business, mentors can help train new employees not only in job functions but in corporate policy and culture. A custom-designed mentoring program can help business achieve these goals with minimal expense and time.

Robert Ferchat, president of Canada's most successful high technology exporters, stresses the value of having mentors to monitor the quality of goods and services. As head of Northern Telecom Canada Ltd., he noted:

> We in North America have long felt that "nobody's perfect" and "isn't one percent error acceptable?" Think for a moment about what it would mean in our daily lives if people got things right only ninety-nine percent of the time: at least two hundred thousand wrong prescriptions would be processed every year; there would be nine misspelled words on every page of a magazine; we'd have unsafe drinking water four times each year; there would be no telephone service for fifteen minutes every day.[2]

Clearly a ninety-nine percent performance does not rank as "good enough" even by our tolerant standards, let alone by those maintained by foreign competitors and customers who regard zero-defect production as absolutely normal. But though the challenge from more quality-conscious producers has long been plain to see, Ferchat said, "We in North America do not *yet* have throughout our culture — outside or inside the corporation — a real, deep, unshakable conviction that quality is the key to competing, the key to survival, the key to growth and profitability."[3]

In the corporate world, mentoring is never a liability. It converts the chain of command into an instrument for developing, enlightening, and inspiring leadership. A president, as mentor, meets with a company's vice presidents to prepare them for larger leadership roles. One on one, the head of the organization shares insights, values, and visions with understudies so they can catch the things that cannot be taught. Vice presidents can in turn hold mentoring meetings with their subordinates to pass along attitudes and actions to unify the leadership team around common purpose and shared values.

In "Managing Your Time" seminars which my colleague Ed Dayton and I have held across the United States and abroad, I teach mentoring as it relates to the development of manpower, resources (money, equipment, property, vehicles, buildings, books, and the Scriptures), information, and experience. These thoughts are subjects of interest to conferees.

Mentoring to Develop Manpower

If an organization is to have a future, it must develop its manpower. The best method of doing that is through the mentoring of its key personnel.

In his book *Iacocca*, the head of the Chrysler Corporation names Charlie Beacham as his primary mentor who taught him to (1) admit his mistakes, (2) get excuses out of the way so he can deal with the problem, and (3) fight the next war, not the last one.[4]

Mal G. King, founder of the Mentor Consulting Group, in Santa Paula, California, believes that, although the ability to lead cannot be taught, it can be intensified through mentoring. It can be "nurtured and honed by in-

fluencing the whole being. And it is precisely this influ-
encing of the whole being that no course, no seminar, no
book can satisfy. It takes life, it takes experience, it takes
contact with a human soul, it takes example, and it takes
emulation. In sum, it takes mentoring."[5]

Charles Colson was born again following the witness
of Tom Phillips, as I mentioned in an earlier chapter.
Chuck was at the very end of his rope, facing his prison
sentence, when Tom gave him the C.S. Lewis classic,
Mere Christianity. A spiritually hungry, desperate Colson
literally devoured the book and, alone with God, gave his
heart to Christ. As a result of careful mentoring by a
choice friend, Chuck in turn has, over the past dozen or
more years, influenced a host of other prisoners, business
leaders, and professionals to open their hearts to Christ.
Having been faithfully mentored himself, Chuck in turn
successfully and most helpfully mentors others.

I asked my friend Bobb Biehl, head of Masterplanning
Group, International, in Laguna Niguel, California, to list
the elements of the mentor-protégé relationship which he
has learned over the years. He wrote:

> When people hear the word *mentor*, they tend to think
> of a white-haired person who is old and feeble, and/or
> rich and famous. And when they hear the word *protégé*,
> they tend to think of a kid on a piano bench learning
> the keyboard from the maestro.

> But in reality, the mentor-protégé relationship in its
> simplest form is a lot like a big brother, big sister rela-
> tionship. The big brother really wants to see the little
> brother win. It isn't that the mentor has to be older.
> But he or she must want very badly to see another per-
> son win, and be committed to helping them win.

A lot of men and women are successful managers. They've managed well their own company, a church, or another type of organization. And good management is what brings that feeling of success. Then deep down inside they begin to think, *I wonder who I could develop and bring along as a protégé.*[6]

Bobb lists these obvious advantages to having a mentor:[7]

- You get to do most things faster if you have a mentor who will *tell* you where to go to find a certain resource or show you how to do something. It's a lot easier to learn when you've got a friend who wants you to develop skill and is teaching you on a one-to-one basis.

- You have available to you the network of the mentor. One of the greatest roles a mentor can play is to introduce a protégé to the right people at the right time.

Many people who are starting out in their business or profession feel as though they are all alone. But a mentoring relationship can give a person the feeling that they have an emotional partner, even though they might not own a piece of the company.

Here are ten suggestions for the mentor, as Bobb sees them, for the relationship with a protégé to "set up right":

1. *The mentor has to remain objective.* If the mentor becomes too involved subjectively, he can ruin the dynamic in the relationship. It is somewhat difficult, for example, for a father to become a mentor to a son or a mother to a daughter. Because the parent is so subjectively involved in the life of a child, it's hard to be objective. A mentor must ask not "How can I make this person feel good?" and not "How can I hype them into thinking they're

wonderful?" and not "How can I criticize them and belittle them to make them shape up?" Instead, the mentor must speak objectively, honestly, candidly for the best interests of the protégé. A mentor must have the honesty to say, "As one of your advisors, this is what I see happening in your life."

2. *Be honest with a protégé.* For example, one of Bobb's male protégés was very much a man but he had feminine gestures. When the time was right, after several hours of just being with him, Bobb decided the time had come to be candid. He actually had to teach his friend how to use his hands and his head. That's an example of raw honesty that was objective enough to help the protégé to see clearly the potential and also the roadblocks keeping him from that potential. It's a little like being a loving Dutch Uncle or Dutch Aunt — someone who will take you aside on occasion and tell you frankly things you need to hear but don't want to hear.

3. *Be a model to a protégé.* Thomas Carlyle's words are worth repeating: "Be what you would have your pupils to be." When I take my associate team along for client consultations I ask them, "What did you learn by watching me as well as by listening to me?" Part of what I am doing as a mentor is teaching my associates by letting them watch me as well as by my telling them what to do.

4. *Be deeply committed to your protégé.* It might be a little bit difficult to see the persons as a younger

brother or sister, particularly if they are older than you. But the Apostle Paul, when writing to his young protégé, Timothy, captured this thought when he said, "If you're working with older men and women, see them as your mother and father. Treat them with the respect that you would want your mother and father to have." If they are younger than you, see them as a younger brother or sister, even though they might not be blood relatives. See them at the level of family commitment.

5. *Be open and transparent.* One of the things that my wife Cheryl has often told me is this: "Your associate team only hears about your successes. Let them hear also about your failures." I have to watch very carefully that I tell my associate team not only when I have won, and when the client has said yes, and when I have given counsel that works, but also when I have failed to win a client, and/or when a bit of advice to a client has not worked.

Every mentor has struggles that the protégé never sees. The protégé might say with some hesitation, "John can do this, but I don't know if I'll ever make it because I have problems with discipline (or doubt, or self-worth, or fatigue)."

Be humble enough to share with a protégé not your dirty laundry, not your skeletons in the closet of thirty years ago, but your struggles today, along with the things you are trying to teach.

6. *Be a teacher.* Many people are unconscious competents. They just do a thing well without knowing

how they do it or exactly what is required to pull it off. At one time they learned how to do a given exercise — an accounting practice, a writing style, a trick of the trade — but have long since forgotten how they do it. If that describes you, write down what you do, why you do it, and how you do it, so that it's transferable.

There are three steps to becoming a teacher:

a. Make a list of ten to fifteen things you are as an individual: disciplined, organized, honest, etc. Then teach those to your protégé.

b. Set down those breakthrough concepts that once a person understands will become powerful servants for the protégé.

c. List the tools you use and show how to use them successfully. These can be anything from psychological profiles to copy machines or tools and services that you handle with ease. When this list is complete, you are in a position to show your protégé what you have learned and how that skill has helped you achieve the success you enjoy today. You have to be able to *teach* these as well as to *model* them by your actions. And you must be able to tell a protégé *why* what you do works, not just to show the protégé that it does work.

7. *Believe in a protégé's potential.* My father-in-law, who is one of my mentors, once introduced me by saying, "I'd like to have you meet my son-in-law, Bobb Biehl." Then he added, "Some day they'll say, 'I'd like to have you meet Joe Kimball, Bobb

Biehl's father-in-law.'" That very thing happened twenty years later in Orlando, Florida.

You have to look at the protégé and say, "Yes, I think this person has tremendous potential. I think if I invest some of my life in him, he has what it takes to be all that he can be."

8. *Envision the protégé's future.* Look into the eyes of your mentoree and see what he feels in his heart but has never thought yet in his head. He might feel like he has tremendous potential but won't allow himself to think that yet. He places limits on himself that the mentor has to eliminate. Help your protégé to see what you feel is his potential, even though he might not yet see it. Put that into words, don't just think it. Tell him, "You have the potential. Go for it!"

Don't hype a person. If he can't carry a tune, don't tell him he will be the star of the Metropolitan Opera some day. There is no substitute for objectivity and honesty. That includes telling a person frankly when he or she has the potential for the endeavor of his or her choice.

9. *You must be successful in the protégé's eyes before he will listen to you.* A protégé must feel that their mentor is the kind of person he or she would like to emulate some day. He or she is successful in what he or she does. He or she is an outstanding leader, etc. That doesn't mean you have to be perfect, just successful at what you do in the eyes of your mentoree.

10. *Be teachable*. This might sound odd as a prerequisite for being a good mentor because it's the *protégé's* job to learn from you. But I have found that if I remain teachable, then I am modeling the teachability which I want my protégé to have. You can learn from everyone. What's more, I've found that as a mentor pours himself into a person and gives and gives and gives, sooner or later that person in whom he has invested so much will want to give him something back.

Let's say I have a whole bunch of oranges. You're thirsty and I give you some of my oranges. Sooner or later you'll want to give something back to me. You might say, "How about a tangerine from me?" If I say, "No, no thank you," that makes it seem as though what I give is valuable but what you give is not. It shuts off the chemistry. But if on the other hand I can learn from you, then suddenly it's a two-way street. The protégé says, "Hey, my mentor respects me" (and vice versa). If the mentor remains teachable, it shows that he really does admire his protégé and believes in his future.[8]

Conclusion: A mentor is a person who believes in the protégé and wants to see him or her win. If you can stay with these ten items and make certain that this is what you bring to the relationship, then you will find that the relationship will set up properly. If you don't have any of these, it's predictable that the relationship will not be satisfying to either party.

"You cannot *not* set an example," is how Mal King of the Mentor Consulting Group puts it.

In an interview for the *Harvard Business Review*, Donald S. Perkins, head of the Jewel Companies, was asked whether he expected mentors to get emotionally involved with protégés. Perkins replied, "If you are asking me if you can work with people without love, the answer is no."

Mal King, in the manuscript for his book *Mentoring, the Only Way To Develop Leaders*, paraphrases Ashley Montagu's definition of love as it applies to mentoring:

> Mentoring is the demonstratively active involvement in the welfare of another in such a way that one not only contributes to the survival of the other, but does so in a creatively enlarging manner, in a manner calculated to stimulate the potentialities of the other so that they may develop to their optimum capacity. It is to communicate to the other that one is profoundly interested in him, that one is there to offer him all the supports and stimulations he requires for the realization of his potentialities for being a person able to relate himself to others in a creatively enlarging manner, who gives the psychological support and sustenance the other requires, to nourish and to enable him to grow not only in his potentialities for being a harmonic being but also to train him in the development of those inner controls that will make external ones unnecessary.[9]

The following story of a mentor and a protégé may be apocryphal, but it tells of a young man who was an apprentice in a bank, rising rapidly in his career. The board of the bank had decided to name him as the new president, to succeed a feisty, crusty old man who had been president of the bank for many years.

One day the young man, who was soon to be president, came into the old man's office and said, "Sir, as you know, I've been appointed by the board to succeed you as president of the bank, and I'd be very grateful for any counsel and help that you could give to me."

The old man said, "Son, sit down. I've got just two words of counsel for you. Two words."

"What are they?"

"*Right decisions.*"

The young man thought a moment and said, "Sir, that's very helpful, but how does one go about making those right decisions?"

The old man responded, "One word."

"And that is?"

"*Experience.*"

"Thank you, sir. I'm sure that'll be helpful. But really, sir, how does one go about gaining experience?"

The old man smiled and said, "Two words. *Wrong decisions.*"

Well, obviously we learn out of our experience, and we make our judgments based upon the experience we garner. And as a good mentor, we can pass along our experiences to others.

Mentoring to Manage Time

A good mentor teaches a mentoree the strategic use of time. The Bible has a great deal to say about this subject. Manpower can be developed, resources can be raised, experience can be gained, and information can be garnered, but time varies not as it passes on to its culmination.

Though utterly irretrievable, time is immensely valuable to the good steward. Undoubtedly it is the most valuable commodity we have. No one has any more time or any less time than the next person. To each of us is given 1,440 minutes of every day, 168 hours in each week. And there are fifty-two weeks in each year.

The clocks we buy and the watches we wear all run at exactly the same rate. Even our Lord, the Creator who left eternity to enter time, lived a very short span of time as we would measure it — thirty-three and a half years.

But think of the quality of the investment in time of our Lord Jesus Christ. And yet in spite of that recognized preciousness and the vast potentiality related to time, there's nothing we squander quite so thoughtlessly as time.

As the wise and pragmatic Sir Walter Scott once wrote: "Dost thou love life, then do not squander time, for that's the stuff life's made of."

Let me suggest to the mentor some characteristics of time worth passing on to a mentoree:

- Time is inelastic, it cannot be expanded or contracted.

- Time dominates everything. Everything requires time. It is expensive and precious, though we treat it as if it were free.

- Time is unique. It cannot be compared to anything else. It stands by itself. There's nothing else like time.

- Time is irreversible. It builds always from the past, through the present, into the future.

- Time means different things at different times to different people.

- Time is always quantifiable, or measurable. We measure it by the rising and setting of the sun. By the tides of the sea. By the phases of the moon. By calendars, by sandclocks, by watches. We have various ways of measuring time, which is very important to us.

- Time is irreplaceable. It has no substitutes. Whereas a computer may at times act as a substitute for individuals, nothing, really, can substitute for time.

- Time is the dimension in which change takes place and motion occurs, in contrast to space.

Of all the resources that are available to both mentor and mentoree, time probably is the most talked about and least understood of those resources.

There are many fallacies that we would readily identify among ourselves concerning this matter of time.

There's the fallacy of activity. The amount of activity squeezed into a given amount of time has very little to do with the results. We dare not let activity become an end in itself. It is not how much we do that counts, but rather it is how much we get done.

There is the fallacy of the delayed decision. The longer a decision is delayed, generally, the more difficult it is to make.

There is the fallacy of the overworked individual: the overworked manager or leader. No one really is indispensable. There's no necessity for anybody, for any length of time, to be overworked.

Then there's the fallacy of hard work. As a resource, time is best spent on "smart," not "hard" work. One of a mentor's goals is to release a mentoree from the bondage of time so that he or she will have more time to do the things that they really want to do.

Biblical Principles of Management

God made man ruler over all the earth (see Genesis 1:26–30). We call this delegated accountability "stewardship."

Biblical examples of good stewards abound in the Bible for the mentoree to emulate. Joshua and Jehoshaphat excelled as military commanders. David and Solomon served as wise administrators of the kingdom of Israel. Joseph and Daniel had the respect of heathen kings as being professional managers of state affairs. Nehemiah, some say, contains all of the major management principles practiced in America today.

In *Hand Me Another Brick,* author Chuck Swindoll calls Nehemiah a classic work on effective leadership. He stresses the importance of the "prayer principle" in Biblical management. Occasionally it is prayer in response to opportunities (see Nehemiah 1:4, 2:5) or prayer in response to opposition (see Nehemiah 4:4).

The prophet Nehemiah knew when to start and also when to get out of the way. Not everyone does. Christian enterprise is filled with people who get a movement off the ground but who couldn't keep it off the ground.

Robert Coleman is the author of the classic work, *The Master Plan of Evangelism.*[10] In it he lists eight principles Jesus used in the discipling of the apostles. They are: (1) selection, (2) association, (3) concentration, (4) impartation, (5) demonstration, (6) delegation, (7) supervision, and (8) reproduction.

Who would not acknowledge that *selection* of the right person for the right job is one of the most important choices a manager can make. That's one reason this book is devoted to the subject of mentoring, so people in the vocations can be all they can be.

The pastor of a famous West Coast church once asked author Bruce W. Jones what he had learned about staff selection. He said he had learned that a pastor needs to be prayerful, patient, and perceptive. The Lord set a good example in taking time and offering many prayers in the selection of His "staff" (see Luke 6:12–13).

A special 1983 edition of *The Harvard Business Review* carries an article titled, "Everyone Who Makes It Has a Mentor." In interviews with three successive chief executives of Jewel Companies, F. J. Lunding, who succeeded the famous John Hancock, stated that he operated his company by "the first assistant philosophy." He went on to explain that this plan means that executive responsibility involves assisting people down the line to be successful in their respective positions. The manager in any department is the first assistant to those who report to him.

Lunding passed this philosophy on to George Clements, who also believed in the mentor philosophy and who then handpicked the current president, Donald Perkins. For Perkins, sponsorship was a lot like parenting. "I don't know that anyone has ever succeeded in any business without having some unselfish sponsorship or mentorship," he said, "whatever it might be called."

In the same publication, there appeared a supporting article titled, "Clues for Success in the President's Job." For the article, author Joseph Bailey interviewed more than thirty top executives. He found that they all learned firsthand from a mentor. Most mentors were positive models, although not all. Occasionally there were some negative examples. In 90 percent of the interviews, these models were successful executives thirty years older, on the average. Each mentor helped the young protégé to form, work out, and practice the patterns of organizational behavior which he or she preferred. A mentor enabled each of them to become good managers. The application of this principle has tremendous implications for the work of God through the Church.

Ed Dayton does not separate the sacred from the secular in management philosophy, believing that there is no more a "Christian" philosophy of management than there is a "Christian" philosophy of bus driving.[11]

Peter Rudge, on the other hand, writes that believers need to apply Christian doctrine to organization and administration in order to develop "managerial theology."

Olan Hendrix holds that the question is not the spirituality of management, but the spirituality of the person who manages.[12]

Bruce Jones concludes in his book, *Ministerial Leadership in a Managerial World*:

> A Biblical philosophy of management simply evaluates the purposes, people, principles, and practices of a church organization by scriptural standards. As such, I believe there can be a Biblical philosophy of management in the broadest sense of the term, even though Christian leaders and pastors will develop distinctive philosophies of management within these broad guidelines.[13]

A Mentor's Quest for Excellence

Above all, a mentor seeks to instill in his charge the pursuit of excellence in service as unto Christ. Two decades ago, Dr. John Gardner, founder of "Common Cause," and author of the best-selling book *Self Renewal*, wrote a book with the simple title of *Excellence*. To this title Dr. Gardner added this subtitle: "Can We Be Equal and Excellent Too?" In it he attacks the idea that it is almost undemocratic to excel in something over our fellow man.

Some may recognize this familiar quote from the book: "The society that scorns excellence in plumbing because plumbing is a humble activity, and tolerates shoddiness in philosophy because it is an exalted activity, will have neither good plumbing nor good philosophy. Neither its pipes nor its theories will hold water."[14]

Dr. Gardner is on the right track. Many of us Christians fall into the same kind of a trap. We become uneasy with the idea of having the best, or being the best, or doing that which is outstanding. Too often we don't mind "excellence" if we can shift responsibility for it onto somebody else. Or, onto the Lord.

"The Lord has really blessed him in his ministry, hasn't he?" we say. Or, "The Lord has really given her great gifts." But we may become suspicious if someone is praised directly for doing an excellent job. I believe that striving for excellence in one's work, whatever it may be, is not only the Christian's duty, but it is a basic form of Christian witness. It might be called the foundation of nonverbal communication which supports the verbal.

Dr. Melvin Lorentzen, for many years connected with the Billy Graham Center at Wheaton College, says in an essay, "We must stress excellence over against mediocrity done in the name of Christ. We must determine to put our best into the arts, so that when we sing a hymn about Jesus and His love, when we erect a building for the worship of God, when we stage a play about the soul's pilgrimage, we will not repel people, but attract them to God."[15]

Dealing with an Impossible Mentor

It is never easy working with a temperamental superior. Nehemiah discovered this as he made plans to return to Jerusalem and rebuild the wall of the city that had broken down through long neglect. Note the steps that the prophet Nehemiah took to accomplish his aims:

First, he continued to undertake his duties as King Artaxerxes' cupbearer cheerfully. He entered the presence of the king each day with a happy countenance as long as he could. When the king noticed that he was downcast, he asked why and then things began to happen in answer to his prayers. In short order, Nehemiah was given permission by the top command to carry out his task (see Nehemiah 2:1–9).

All went well until Sanballat the Horonite and Tobiah the Ammonite heard about the venture and opposed it. But Nehemiah was prepared with letters from King Artaxerxes and hurdled one obstacle after another because he had planned ahead (see Nehemiah 2:7–10).

Charles Swindoll gave his congregation at The Evangelical Free Church of Fullerton, California, these four timeless principles for dealing with discouragement:

1. Changing a heart is God's specialty, no matter how stubborn a superior might be. Don't try to do it yourself. Don't manipulate, trick, or deceive them. God will take care of them for your good.

2. Praying and waiting go hand in hand. You haven't prayed until you've learned to wait. And you haven't prayed until you've prayed with release.

3. Faith is not a synonym for disorder or a substitute for careful planning. People of faith have orderly minds. Leaders, like Nehemiah, think through each situation. Though their circumstances allow them to go through only the first step, they have

thought through the next twelve. Faith breeds organization.

4. Opposition, instead of hindering, often reinforces the will of God. It's probably not the will of God unless someone vehemently opposes your plan.[16]

Take a cue from Nehemiah:

> He faces financial needs,
>   so he asks the king for letters.
> He's afraid, so he prays for the words to say.
> He's a man of faith, yet he makes careful plans.
> He's a man of qualified courage,
>   yet he got on his mount anyway and took off.[17]

And best of all, he never forgot:

> The king's heart is in the hand
>   of the LORD;
>   he directs it like a watercourse
>   wherever he pleases.
>   (Proverbs 21:1)

Cross-Cultural Mentoring

To writer Tim Stafford, a key ingredient in a successful mentoring relationship is the eagerness of the person to be mentored. Tim made the comment following his experiences in Kenya where he started a magazine and trained its writers and editors.[18]

The atmosphere of his monthly editorial workshops were unlike anything he had ever experienced in the United States. "In the states," he recalled, "people come to seminars with a jaded palate. The leaders are always on trial. They must prove that they can justify their use of

others' time. I'm not knocking that; I take a similar attitude myself."

But in Kenya, would-be writers came early and stayed
late. They listened "as though gold might come out of my
mouth. It was actually a little frightening to be attended
to with such intensity: what if I casually said something
that led them astray? I had to become as serious about my
role as they were about theirs."

One of Tim's protégés stands out among the rest. He is
Haron Wachira, a young and unformed man who spoke
with an atrocious rural accent when he first came to the
Saturday workshop. Tim saw at once that he was quite talented and that he had an enormous appetite for learning.

Eventually Tim hired the young man to be his assistant editor at *Step*, the magazine he was launching. They
shared a tiny office — so tiny that their knees almost
bumped. Every day they ate lunch together at a dirt-floor,
cardboard-walled kiosk down the road.

"I've had other mentoring relationships where we met
infrequently," Tim said, "but they just didn't match the
intensity possible when you're together that much. There
are soon no secrets. You are not as much 'teaching' as
you are living. The learning went in both directions, too.
He absorbed my life, personally as well as professionally; I
absorbed his."

The two men culturally came from different worlds
and had to learn a great deal just to understand each
other. Because they were together so much of the time for
the the work at hand, and because Wachira wanted so
much to learn, their differences were only a minor aspect
of their many points of contact. Ultimately, they left behind the mentoring relationship and became simply
friends and colleagues.

"Wachira remains one of my closest personal friends," says Tim, "someone I can talk to for days on end just as I did in that tiny office ten years ago."

In the 1940s, Norman Vincent Peale arrived in Chicago by train to speak at three important meetings. He was the first person to disembark at the station where he quickly engaged a porter to carry his two large suitcases and urged him, "Please bring those bags quickly."

Happy to be ahead of the other passengers, Peale started off at a fast clip toward the street. Suddenly he noticed that his porter was not following. "Come *on*," he urged. "I'm late."

The porter, not increasing his speed, said, "Where you steamin' for, brother? That aint no way to make time." Then he added calmly, "Just walk on ahead and I'll come along, and there won't be two minutes between us."

As the great writer, speaker, and promoter of life-enrichment experiences walked alongside the baggage truck, the porter preached him a sermon. The gist was: "Take it easy. You can do a lot in a short time if you just go along easy at it. Besides," he added, "you'll live longer."

Peale told the man he was a preacher and that he was going to take his idea to the pulpit on Sunday. "Do you go to church?" he asked the porter.

"Yes sir, I do," he said. And then he finished off the traveler completely by adding, ". . . and I try to practice what I hear there."[19]

Albert W. Balzer, a builder who left a thriving enterprise in southern California, spent nearly thirty years as a lay missionary in the Central African Republic with the Foreign Missions Society of the Brethren Church. He was unusually adept at getting the Africans to work hard in the building of new churches throughout the country. What was his secret?

"The key to working with the African brothers," he says, "is having trust in them. My wife Elsie, for example, was the only homemaker on our compound who let the African boy plan and cook the meals."[20]

The other key factors, Balzer said, were letting the Africans supervise their own people and giving them responsibility. Al would start new workers on an hourly wage agreed upon and then watch carefully how many bricks they made each hour. After he determined how many they could make in an hour, he would double the quota required daily, put them on piece work, and let them stop when their quota was finished. Under that plan, the Africans worked hard, completed their allotment by noon, then went home to enjoy the afternoon with their families. Everyone was happy. The name of Al Balzer is still revered among those Africans still living in the C.A.R.

Mentoring in the Military

"Mentoring" for the purpose of conducting warfare is well known to me. I served in World War II first in an artillery unit and later with the Military Police in Camp Young near Palm Springs, California. In the years since I was in the service as a sergeant, the U.S. Army has established a mentorship-based strategy. Its purpose is to develop an officer corps that has the knowledge, skills, abilities, and character to be able both to think about the conduct of war in broad terms and to adapt to the demands of a fast-paced tactical environment.

The armed forces have shown that they can take *anybody* and train them to do just about anything. To reach

his goals, a soldier is mentored. He is shown. They start
the mentoring process by assigning to you what you *can*
do and take you to what you didn't know you could do. I
know of no other agency that does as good a job of
mentoring as the military because of its hands-on style.
To form a band of men into a fighting unit, the military
takes pluralistic fears and turns them into a unified, controlled aggression.

Mentoring in the military teaches a responsive lifestyle. To get a mentoree to respond, you must get beyond
their reaction. If people are afraid, they react; if they are
distraught, they react. The mentoree must be trained so
that he is in control of his circumstances. This comes
down to the Biblical definition of meekness: "Power
under control."

I remember my sergeant in basic training. His name
was Joe Petulo. He was with us *all* the time — up early in
the morning, up late at night . . . he was on the march
with us. He went through the exercises with us. He always
looked spit-and-polish clean. Always a model. And there
were times when he would put it to us when we thought
we couldn't make it. And there were other times when he
would take a guy who was crying and couldn't pull himself
together, and he would treat him with tender concern. We
all had a love-hate relationship with this fellow.

"I'm here to train you because I want you to come
home to your parents, your wives, your kids," he would
say. "I don't want you to come home in a coffin. And the
only way is to get you conditioned to fight combat cor-
rectly. You can't be selfish. If you think you're the center
of the universe, listen, you're dead. Your buddy and your
weapon and your company and this country come before
you. Think about it."

In the U.S. Navy, Admiral Chester W. Nimitz was known to run a tight ship, but he was also famous for creating an excellent environment for learning among his men. Even mistakes and failure would not necessarily result in a destroyed career for those under the famous admiral.

One day as his ship steamed into port, he called up an unsuspecting ensign, as he usually did, "to the bridge to berth the ship." It was only the ensign and Nimitz up there on the bridge as the critical maneuver took place.

The admiral watched the rookie without saying a word as the young officer aimed the ship at port. The young man, it was obvious, was in the process of charging the dock at a rapid pace. Nimitz bit his tongue because he could see the impact coming. At the last critical second the ensign, realizing he had a problem, commanded full reverse and docked the ship beautifully.

When he was walking away after all lines were tied and the ship secure, Nimitz asked the young ensign what he thought he did wrong. The young ensign indicated that he recognized he was coming in much too rapidly. Captain Samuel S. Robison afterward said he was certain that Nimitz would have taken full responsibility, blaming himself and not the ensign for the collision.[21]

The literature on the techniques of mentoring in the military seems to be endless. Soldiers and sailors who desire to become mentors and sponsors and promoters are encouraged to read Martin Blumenson's description of Patton in the *Patton Papers*.

> He attracted his superiors by his enthusiasm, his devotion to his profession, his willingness to learn, his serious application, his loyalty to his seniors, his concern for the welfare of his subordinates, his meticulous at-

tention to orders and the job, his neatness in dress and appearance, his military bearing and good looks, his pleasant personality, and his adaptability.[22]

Tributes to Life-Changers

Most successful people, when asked to name a mentor, can do so without hesitation. Some can name more than one. Except for the first testimonial below, which has been published in a book, the following are informal responses from friends about their mentors:

"A Billion-Dollar Friend" by Fred Smith, President, Fred Smith Associates

Maxey Jarman took a company from seventy-five employees to seventy-five thousand, making Genesco in the late sixties the world's largest apparel company, doing over a billion dollars in sales. I joined him in 1941 when the company had five thousand employees and was doing less than one hundred million dollars. When reverses came, Maxey maintained a tremendous spiritual resiliency and kept contributing energetically, without bitterness, to many Christian causes. He was a man who rose to the very top in business, yet was uncompromising in his spiritual commitments. He inspired me in high times and in low times alike. He was always, for me, a living lesson.

I first met Maxey Jarman back in the mid-thirties when I was about twenty years old. I had been teaching a Sunday school class in a nurses' training program at Nashville General Hospital. One of the nurses became an industrial nurse, and she introduced me to her boss, the director of personnel. I said to myself, "I'd like a job like that." I had no training or experience, but I knew General Shoe (later Genesco) was one company in town where there might be such a position. So, I decided to meet Maxey Jarman, the president.

I met him at a Rexall drug store. We sat on fountain stools drinking cokes, and he asked me what I planned to do in life. "I'd like to be a personnel man," I told him. He asked if I'd ever had any experience, and I said, "No, I've never even seen a personnel department. But I met a guy who's a personnel man, and I think I'd like that kind of work."

That night I told Mary Alice, my wife, I thought he would offer me a job, and no matter what he offered, I was going to take it because he was a man I wanted to be associated with.

I had never seen a man so serious about wanting to reach the truth. . . . I've learned much from Maxey. He had an awesome sense of responsibility. Maxey was cause-oriented. Maxey was future-oriented. Maxey differentiated between gossip and grapevine. Time was Maxey's greatest "means." Maxey looked first at opportunities. Maxey implemented responsibility with a strong, consistent discipline. Maxey never became cynical. Maxey was a much better demonstrator than a teacher. Money to Maxey was a means, not an end.

He built a billion-dollar corporation, but neither success nor failure was crucial to his interior life. He treated "those two impostors" just the same. Maxey Jarman was not a talking-teacher—he was a living example, which made him one of my cherished mentors.[23]

"Helen of Light and Life" by Vera Bethel, Editor, Free Methodist Publishing House
   I think often of all the fun I had with my mentor, Helen Hull, a superb editor and a gracious lady to all her

writers and artists. One of the biggest things I learned was not to take oneself too seriously.

One day Helen and I disagreed with our supervisor, Don Joy, quite strongly. Then later, we found out we were wrong. So we got down on our hands and knees, crawled out of our office, down the hall of the headquarters building, into his office and right up to his desk to beg forgiveness. Helen was impulsive like I am and less inhibited. She was always willing to do crazy things.

From her I learned to sort out the interesting manuscripts from the boring ones. I learned a little bit about how to teach aspiring writers a few clues about writing and marketing. We laughed together all the time; sometimes I wondered how we got any work done. But creativity flourishes best in an atmosphere of fun—and we had plenty of that. The only thing she took really seriously was her relationship with God. Pomposity in the tiniest degree amused her; she just took everything lightly.

"Teacher" by Bill Bright, President, Campus Crusade for Christ, Inc.

It was a Wednesday evening. Dr. Henrietta C. Mears had just finished her Bible study and a young man approached her asking for counsel. At that time I was the president of the college-age/postcollege group and found myself unintentionally overhearing the conversation. And then it appeared that, with a few well-chosen questions, Dr. Mears had perceived that this young man was really hungry for God. And so she began to explain to him how he could become a Christian.

I sat quietly over to the side listening and praying. But that night, through her modeling experience, I had opportunity to observe one of the reasons God used her so mightily. Here was one who could speak with great brilliance and the anointing of God's Spirit to multitudes, but she was also concerned for the individuals.

The Bible reminds us that God is not willing that any should perish, but that all should come to repentance. Jesus has commissioned us to go into all the world and make disciples of all nations. "Follow Me and I will make you fishers of men" (Matthew 4:19). The absolute number one priority of every believer is to be available to God's Holy Spirit to win and disciple the lost. Jesus said, "Ye shall receive power, after that the Holy Ghost is come upon you; and ye shall be witnesses unto me both in Jerusalem, and in all Judaea, and in Samaria, and unto the uttermost part of the earth" (KJV Acts 1:8).

Dr. Mears knew the reality of the Spirit-anointed, controlled life. Dr. Mears was not only a good teacher, but she was also an excellent model.

"Dear Mentor . . ." (A letter to Milford Sholund, upon his retirement as Director of Publications at Gospel Light Publications) by Fritz Ridenour, Editorial Project Developer, Freelance

When you work with someone for seventeen years and nine months, you have a lot of things to remember, and a few things you'd like to forget. I remember . . .

How happy you were when I came to work for G/L in 1959. You had only been here a few years and didn't have that much clout. You weren't even "doctor" yet, so you were glad to see me, because that made two males on the top floor at 725 Colorado, where G/L was headquartered at the time.

Of course I'll always remember your sense of discipline. In fact, so impressed have I been by your devotion to duty that I have seen fit to fondly call you Moses, while I have tried in some faint and shadowy way to perform like Joshua.

And no matter how hot the battle, you never let me falter. I remember especially how I stood before your desk weeping and begging for mercy, saying I could not go on with the high school curriculum. We had already done five or six courses and I had written as many paperback books. I was tired; I was spent; I was drained of creative energies. As the tears trickled off the end of my nose, I bleated, "I gotta have a rest. I can't do it. . . . I can't go on!"

You just smiled and said understandingly, "Go on. . . . "

Early in my career, I trembled when my manuscripts would come back from your desk. Every dog-ear was worth at least a few minutes of discussion and/or rebuke. But that was how we all learned. Grappling with those dog-ears made us experts in doctrine, grass-roots theology and . . . your parables. . . .

You may be going, at least in part, Moses, but you are far from forgotten. Like Joshua, I face a future filled with pressures. Joshua looked across the Jordan and saw walled cities, spears, swords, and battles ahead. For me, it's more deadlines, more dog-ears, more memos, more meetings, and more battles ahead.

If you taught me anything, it was the reality of God being with me wherever I go. In so many ways you have been like a father to me. You saw my mistakes and corrected me. You recognized my weaknesses and disciplined me. But through it all I always felt you cared about me — and I came to care about you.

It is said we all stand on the shoulders of others. I certainly stand on the strong Swedish shoulders of Sholund, the farm boy from Gothenburg, who traveled far, learned much, and ministered to so many. You certainly ministered to me. The books that I have written were done only because of your steady guiding hand. You have been my teacher, my critic, my biggest fan, my father, my friend.

And these things I will not forget.

"Peacemaker in Blue" by Robert L. Vernon, Assistant Chief of Police, Los Angeles Police Department

The greatest mentor in my life was my father. He was an officer in the Los Angeles Police Department in the days when members of the force had only four days off each month, one day a week, yet he would spend a lot of that time with me rather than doing things with other men.

One day I rode home on my bike with a new reflector mounted on the frame. My father noticed it immediately. I think that's significant because he was very much aware of my property.

"Bob," he said, "where did you get that reflector?"

I said, "I got it from Donald for fifteen cents."

"Well, where did Donald get it?"

"Donald stole it," I told my dad, not thinking anything about it because I didn't know it was stolen until after I had mounted it on my bike.

"Are you telling me you have stolen property there, Pal?" my dad asked.

"Dad, you don't understand," I said in my eight-year-old rationalization. "I had nothing to do with stealing the reflector."

He took me into the garage of our house in Lincoln Heights, and invited me to sit down on an orange crate to talk this over. "I'm not going to punish you, Son," he began, "because I can see that you don't think you've done anything wrong. Let's just talk this time."

My father put the situation into terms a kid could understand. "Now, let's see," he began, "you had to cut Mrs. Stanley's lawn for three weeks in order to get enough money to buy that sheepskin seat you have on your bike, right? Now, what if that kid at the end of the street who steals from everybody, what if he steals your sheepskin seat off the bike and gives it to your best buddy, Albert Casino, who lives next door. When you approach Albert about it, he says, 'Wait a minute, I had nothing to do with this. I didn't tell him to steal it. He didn't even tell me it was stolen until after I got it on my bike." (Dad cleverly used my same words in telling this hypothetical situation.)

I began agreeing with my father that it was wrong to have something that didn't belong to you. That incident, which happened nearly half a century ago, taught me a valuable lesson about respecting other people's property.

That afternoon, Dad drove me over to Donald's house where I gave him back the reflector. A couple of the guys there heard me give it back and called me a sissy. I was feeling pretty low.

Then en route home, my father took me down to Olympic and Soto Streets and took me into the automotive section of Sears and Roebuck store. "Now," he said, "pick out any reflector you want."

Instead of getting a fifteen-center, I picked out one that must have cost a couple of bucks—one of those truck reflectors that had marbles in it and everything.

That was a prized jewel on my bike. "You have that," my father told me, "because you told the truth and tried to make things right."

That whole experience took about four hours out of my dad's time on a Saturday afternoon. It was more than merely giving rules or verbal direction; it was mentoring in the finest manner.

The recurring theme in all of these testimonials by mentors is that of *thanksgiving.* "To receive honestly," wrote George MacDonald, "is the best thanks for a good thing."[24] In response, let each mentor echo the sentiments of the Apostle Paul: "I will very gladly spend for you everything I have and expend myself as well" (2 Corinthians 12:15).

The true mentor defends his pupil against his own personal influence. He inspires self-trust. He guides their eyes from himself to the spirit that quickens him. He will have no disciples.

Amos Bronson Alcott
1799–1888

SEVEN

WOMEN AS MENTORS

Likewise, teach the older women . . . what is good. Then they can train the younger women to love their husbands and children, to be self-controlled and pure, to be busy at home, to be kind, and to be subject to their husbands, so that no one will malign the word of God.

Titus 2:3–5

As the husband of one woman for fifty years, a brother to a sister, the father of a daughter, the member of a board chaired by a woman, and as the co-worker of hundreds, perhaps thousands, of women down through the years in the work of the Lord, I feel qualified to write about the lofty and inexhaustible legacy of God to mentoring women. I concur with the sentiments of Leon Bloy, an instigator of Renaissance thinking in France, who wrote, "The holier a woman is, the more she is a woman."[1] Through Christ, women receive full human rights as man's companion and helpmate. As moral personalities, neither was subordinate but each perfected by the other. As a wife serves her husband, so a husband serves his wife.

Women Mentors in the Bible

Throughout the Scriptures, God's plan for women is revealed in their sovereign exploits as they march through its pages. Eve, the first woman, grew closer to God in the later years of her motherhood, having given birth to and "mentored" the people at the fountainhead of the human race. She said at the birth of her last named son, Seth, "God has granted me another child in place of Abel, since Cain killed him" (Genesis 4:25). And when Eve's grandson Enos was born to Seth, "At that time men began to call on the name of the LORD" (Genesis 4:26).

Jochebed, the mother of Moses, was the member of a priestly family (see Numbers 26:59). This godly woman probably did not live to see her son become one of Israel's spiritual giants, but she recognized that he was born to a high destiny when he was only a baby. It was Jochebed, without doubt, who summoned her other children to excellence — her son Aaron, the first head of the Hebrew priesthood, and her daughter, Miriam, who sang to God as she led the women of Israel across the Sea of Reeds as if it were dry land.

Sarah, the wife of Abraham and the mother of Isaac, was called "blessed" by her children and grandchildren.

Rebekah, in her maidenhood, was chaste and thoughtful, willing to sacrifice all for what was morally right.

Naomi had an intimate contact with God. When she learned how kindly her kinsman Boaz had treated her son's widow, Ruth, on the first days she worked in his field as a gleaner, Naomi prayed out loud, "The LORD bless him. . . . [He] has not stopped showing his kindness to the living and the dead" (Ruth 2:20).

Ruth herself is described in the various translations as "a woman of worth," "virtuous," and "of noble character." Before he married her, Boaz commended her because, as a widow, she had not "run after the younger men, whether rich or poor" (Ruth 3:10).

Hannah, the woman with a sorrowful spirit because she had had no son, never forgot God in her many trials. She would later be clothed with strength and honor, which is of far greater significance than to say she was the richest woman in Israel or that she ruled over it with an iron will, as did the hated Athaliah.

The New Testament includes many accounts of women in the ministry of Christ. Elizabeth, the mother of John the Baptist, surely was a mentor to Mary, the mother of our Lord. Mary paid her a visit and stayed for three months. During that time she must have watched with interest just how a godly couple related to each other in marriage.

Dee Brestin, winner of *Decision's* Achievement Award at its School of Christian Writing for her book *The Friendships of Women*, wondered about Mary's staying with another family for such a long time — three months. She asked Win Couchman, a retreat speaker on the subject of cross-generational relations, what she thought. Win, who said having a Filipino daughter-in-law helped her to understand the story of Mary and Elizabeth, noted:

> Lengthy visits away from fiancé or husband seemed so natural to her. And especially natural would be the visit between two pregnant relatives. There is an ex-

tremely open sharing between women in a family that I have been learning, to my delight, from this precious provincial woman. Her view of time is so different. Three months? A short visit.[2]

Mrs. Brestin included in her book an interesting debate in England concerning the giving of contraceptives to teenagers. The negative viewpoint was taken by an eloquent English mother. She said that encouraging teens in premarital sex uses up their "balm." She explained that during the difficult first year of marriage, when a couple is adjusting to each other, they need that balm of tremendous sexual excitement to soothe the hurts they unintentionally inflict on each other. Mary and Joseph had not used up their balm, nor would they be using it, as there were to be no sexual relations until after Jesus was born. Mary and Joseph were going to need, instead, the balms of kindness, tenderness, and trust in God.

"I believe," says Dee, "God built up this balm in Mary by providing her with a mentor, by having her spend three months with a devout older woman who showed respect and love for her husband."

Many were the women in the life of our Lord: The Canaanite woman whose persistence earned her His respect and praise—the woman of great faith who had an issue of blood—Mary and Martha, the sisters of Lazarus who provided an interesting study in contrasts—and Mary the harlot.

After the Church was born and Christ's disciples were covering the earth with the gospel, Priscilla stood side by side with her husband Aquila in offering spiritual counsel and guidance to Apollos, the young preacher.

The New Testament's finest chapters on womanhood appear in the First Letter of Paul to Timothy and in the Letter of Paul to Titus in his instruction for women in the church. Paul advises women to be "worthy of respect, not malicious talkers but temperate and trustworthy in everything" (1 Timothy 3:11). The New English Bible translates the passage beautifully: "Their wives, equally, must be women of high principle, who will not talk scandal, sober and trustworthy in every way." What a beautiful way to describe that invisible armor of women of high principle that is impenetrable.

The Apostle Paul, who does not always flatter women, wrote in 2 Timothy 3:6–7 about women who are "weak-willed . . . who are loaded down with sins and are swayed by all kinds of evil desires, always learning but never able to acknowledge the truth."

In his letter to Titus, probably from Macedonia, Paul set up modes of conduct for aged women. These reach a high point in Christian behavior. He counsels them to be "reverent in the way they live, not to be slanderers or addicted to much wine, but to teach what is good" (Titus 2:3).

Women Mentors of History

Women have had important roles in mentoring in the millenia of history since the Church was born. They share their exploits with the most famous of men. Here are a few taken from assorted literature and history texts, including *The Bible's Legacy for Womanhood* by Edith Deen.[3]

In *The Divine Comedy*, Dante, the great prophetic exponent of the heart of the Middle Ages, leaned heavily upon Beatrice. She was his ideal guide through Paradise, and Dante saw the Creator because Beatrice's eyes were upon God.

In his eulogy to his saintly mother, Monica, St. Augustine tells how, by her example, she rescued him from sin and how, by her influence, she directed his mind from things transitory to things eternal.

In the early Church, Jerome the scribe was aided and inspired in his translation of the Bible by the noble Roman woman Paula and her daughter Eustochium. Paula often worked right beside Jerome as he did his translation from the original Hebrew and Greek texts into the Latin Vulgate in the Holy Land, where she is buried. Jerome dedicated some of his Bible books and commentaries to Paula and Eustochium, whom he called his spiritual daughters.

Michelangelo had for encouragement one of the noble spirits of the Italian Renaissance — the lovely Vittoria Colonna, who increased his religious faith and inspired him with an ideal of womanhood.

In science, the Latin physicist and astronomer Galileo was inspired by his loving daughter Celeste. Pasteur, the French bacteriologist, had the help of his devoted wife. Jean Louis Agassiz, the celebrated Swiss-American naturalist, owed much to his wife, Elizabeth Cary Agassiz, who was president of Radcliffe College and also remembered because she held her students to the highest ideals of womanhood. John Stuart Mill, the English writer, logician, and economist, spoke from experience when he declared, "Hardly anything can be of greater value to a man of theory and speculation who employs himself, not in collecting materials of knowledge by observation, but in working them up by processes of thought into comprehensive truths of science and laws of conduct than to carry on his speculations in the companionship and under the criticism of a really superior woman."[4]

Devout women mentors today are calling others of their gender to seize the greatness and decency taken from them in the debased "new" sex standards (or lack of standards), in pornographic literature, lurid sex films, and other decaying modes of morality which accentuate the most depraved instincts in womanhood.

Women Mentors in the Workplace

There are an estimated forty-three million women in the American work force. These have a median age of thirty-four and constitute more than two-fifths of the workers. A total of sixty-two percent of all adult women work, in comparison with eighty-eight percent of all men. Most are in lower-paying, dead-end jobs where they earn about three-fifths of what men do. Women workers with a college degree often earn less than men who never went past the eighth grade. Women in professional fields earn salaries that are closer to that of men, but even these women are at the lower end of the pay scale.

Women hold only six percent of top-level administrative positions. An even smaller number of women are in other large organizational positions of real power, such as corporate board members, presidents, key vice presidents, controllers of the purse strings, or even managers of large numbers of people or other resources. Why? Could it be that women have not been given the encouragement, training, or coaching to compete successfully in the professional world?

Nancy W. Collins, the assistant to the president of the Palo Alto Medical Foundation in California, wrote of her experiences:

> I have learned that for an ambitious woman, such as myself, a mentor is even more crucial to her career than to her male counterpart's. Looking back on my own working life, I realize that I have had a new mentor about every eight to ten years. All have been men, and all were ten to fifteen years older. The relationship with each one was different and necessary for that stage of my personal growth and development.[5]

Ms. Collins had three mentors in the course of her professional life. She met her first after graduating from the University of North Carolina and while working for a large Fortune 500 corporation where her mentor was a senior vice president. She did not work directly for him and stayed with the company for only a short time. However, by his own purpose and professional example, her mentor helped to shape her personal philosophy and to formulate her desire to have a serious career, not merely a job. The mentor she chose was one who was greatly revered throughout the organization, who took the time to show an interest in the growth and development of younger people, and taught her to "think big," and to see the whole picture.

Ms. Collins' second mentor was director of a program in which she became the assistant director, at the Stanford University Graduate School of Business. This mentor selected her and gave her an opportunity to put into action certain skills and strategies that she had been accumulating. He assigned to her total responsibility for some segments of the program, saying that in these areas "the buck stops with you." It remained unsaid, but the mentor let her know that he was always there with loyalty and support.

Her third and final mentor relationship occurred when Ms. Collins was in her early forties. This influential man was a CPA in San Francisco. They never worked together, but the mentor helped her get her career in focus. He offered "excellent advice" on making a job change, and the shove that made her do it. She learned from mentor number three the importance of taking advantage of unexpected opportunities as they come along. He was someone with whom she could do "reality testing" with: Were her ideas good ones? How were others perceiving her?

This mentor was so pleased that she mentioned him in her book that he sent the following quote, which has the sentiments expressed in a story earlier in this book: "Good judgment comes from experience, good experience comes from bad judgment."

It is important for a protégé during a traumatic work time to have someone believe in him, to reinforce his belief in himself, and to say that not only does he know you will survive but that you will land on your feet in an even higher place.

Recipes for Success in Vocational Mentoring

As a man with half a century of experience working with women in office situations, I have the following suggestions for her success as a mentor in the field of business:

1. *Obey your intuition.* Cool, calculating, rational thought is characteristic of men in business but

women add an important new dimension: a well-honed facility called intuition.

Peter Drucker, Tom Peters, and a number of other writers have described the superior management style of the Japanese in using intuition successfully. Analysis is fine, they say, when it provides the foundation for intuition. My wife says that women pay attention to details often overlooked by men, making a woman more thoughtful and accommodating in her associations. This is an enormous asset in the mentoring process on the job.

2. *Dress appropriately as a woman.* Women who wear men's clothing might give the wrong impression. Others in the office might think that a woman really wants to be "superior," and to be a man "when she grows up."

3. *Use love to develop a protégé.* Because of a woman's capacity to love, she is well-suited to develop leaders through mentoring. Since mentoring is the involvement of one person in the welfare of another so that the potentialities of the other are developed to their optimum capacity, the special and creative care of a woman can hasten the process.

Henry Adams believed that most successful men owed more to the American woman than to all the American men he ever heard of. He declared in *The Education of Henry Adams* that woman was the superior of the genders. "Apart from truth," he said, "he owed her at least that compliment."[6]

4. *Don't compete with men.* Rather than to compete with men, a mentor is advised to compete against her own best self. Ashley Montagu reminds: "Woman is the creator and fosterer of life; man has been the mechanizer and destroyer of life."[7]

In the final analysis, mentoring in general, and specifically as it involves women, does not easily lend itself to a definition of its components. It's a little like trying to define what constitutes a friend or what a friend "does." The relationship is formal and impersonal, yet constructive and of great use. Perhaps the most valuable thing a mentor does is to help the young person grasp the difference between what's really important and what only seems so. The word for this would be *perspective*.

Gail Sheehy, author of the famous book *Passages*, wrote an article for *New York Magazine* titled: "The Mentor Connection: The Secret Link in the Successful Woman's Life."[8] In her research she stressed the importance of successful women having one or more mentors. She also stated frankly that women have a harder time finding mentors than men do. She found, as did Nancy W. Collins, that successful women had, at some point in their professional lives, the nurturing of a mentor.

In *Mentors and Protégés*, Linda Phillips-Jones gives many examples of experienced career women who were eager to encourage less-experienced women. One of the women described was Katherine S. White, the late fiction editor of *The New Yorker*, who was known for the unshakable faith she had in her writers and who nurtured them as they went on to better writing.

"When White died," said Ms. Phillips-Jones, "the magazine was deluged with letters that praised her and described the profound effect that her deep sense of caring had on people's lives."[9]

Mentoring Within the Family

Within the structure of the family unit, a mother, a mother-in-law, a sister, an aunt, or another relative can quite naturally become a mentor to another. Women are more tightly knit within the family structure than men are. There is some truth to the couplet that James C. Dobson quotes in a film series of Focus on the Family:

> A son is a son 'til he takes a wife,
> But a daughter's a daughter for the rest of her life.

Because of their gift for nurturing relationships, women are less likely to abandon their parents emotionally. They're more faithful, generally speaking, in writing, calling, visiting, and expressing love for their parents.

When her sister lost her mother-in-law, a writer noted the grief that was expressed by the bereaved. Her sister said of her departed mother-in-law:

Everybody loved Lillian! Just being near her was a comfort and a lift. Her humor, her joy in life, her attentiveness to your thoughts and feelings, her quiet faith. Lillian spent three months living with us one time. My friends raised their eyebrows and said, "Three months? Three months with your mother-in-law in the same house?" But it wasn't a difficult time. It is a joyous precious memory in our lives. It helped that she was sensitive to both my need for privacy and my need for help. She would take long walks. She would completely stay out of the kitchen during preparation time. She said two cooks was one too many — so instead she would talk to the kids. I liked that. Then, afterward, she would insist on cleaning up by herself. I was drawn to her because of the way she loved me. . . .[10]

Conference speaker Win Couchman suggests that younger women take the lead in intiating a mentor relationship with older women — asking to spend time, asking to observe. . . . It could begin with a simple request such as asking for help in making an apple pie or in balancing a budget. It may begin by the younger woman asking the older woman to share some of her wisdom.

Older women aren't much different from young women. Many are the beautiful stories of relationships bridging the generations. Unfortunately, some churches permanently divide adult Sunday school classes according to age. This makes it difficult for the older women to teach the younger, as the Apostle Paul admonishes in Titus 2:3–5.

Although it is best for younger women to initiate the mentor relationship, the exceptions can prove the rule. Shortly after Steve Brestin had finished medical school and taken his wife Dee to his first practice, Mrs. Brestin received a call from a woman named Beryl.

"Are you Dr. Brestin's wife?" asked the voice on the phone.

When Dee answered in the affirmative the caller went on to say, "I want you to know I'm in love with your husband." Then she broke into the shocked silence with a warm, loving laugh. "I also want you to know," she said, "I'm old enough to be his mother."

Beryl went on to explain that she had prayed fervently in the ambulance as she sat next to her stricken mother, asking God to send them a compassionate, patient doctor.

"Your husband," she said, "was God's gracious answer to my prayer."

Beryl showed the young wife an open door of friendship. She also showed the young newcomer God's love, joy, and patience as Dee watched her delight in her twenty-eight-year-old son who has Down's syndrome.

Adds Dee: "We can sing with feeling, 'What a Friend We Have in Jesus!' But it is also true, especially in the model of an older woman who has allowed God to spin her on His potter's wheel, to say with feeling, 'What a Jesus We Have in a Friend!'"[11]

David and Karen Mains are heard on the Chapel of the Air radio broadcast nationwide. Karen recounted the story one day of a seventy-year-old nun who cleaned her house when Karen was a young mother. The only payment Sister Theresa would accept was that of bus fare. Every time the clock hit the quarter hour, Sister Theresa would pray — the discipline was so well engrained into the fabric of her life.

"I think of her now with tears," says Mrs. Mains. "I am certain that Sister Theresa built something into my life that I'm beginning to reap and see the benefit of now."[12]

Vonette Bright, co-founder with her husband Bill of Campus Crusade for Christ, recalls how the busy wife of her pastor at the First Presbyterian Church of Hollywood shared with her the richness of her life in frequent encounters.

Marie Evans is the wife of the late Dr. Louis Evans Sr., who was my pastor when Bill and I became members there. She was mother to four children and also a busy grandmother.

She sat in the same pew at church for Sunday services
so that her husband always knew where to find her.
She is such a well-groomed, beautifully dressed, cul-
tured, elegant lady with a queenly manner, though very
loving, friendly and compassionate, just as I have
hoped to look at the same age. I would call her the
epitome of the Proverbs 31 woman. She has helped me
see that chapter not as written by "a mother-in-law,"
but as a possible, attainable goal.

One evening Bill brought home some brains and asked
for eggs and brains for supper. I phoned my pastor's
wife and she had a recipe. That was only one of many
calls to Mrs. Evans from a young homemaker.

Thank you, Marie. I love you.[13]

Ruth Norman, R.N., was a tall woman, free with her
gestures and quite outspoken. She directed the medical
services of a Denver, Colorado unified school and never
knew a stranger. Ruth was continually reaching out in
love to mentor those who came within her domain.

When she spotted Nancy Witham, a thin kindergarten teacher in her school fresh from the university, Ruth
invited her to dinner. Nancy hesitated a moment, remem-
bering that she could not drive a car, but then gratefully
accepted.

She asked her roommate to drive her to Ruth's house
but regretted it when her driver lost her way, became
furious, swore, slammed doors, and let it be known that
she was sorry she had ever accepted the assignment. They
were two hours late when their car finally rolled up at its
destination. Nancy had grown smaller and smaller in the
car and had to screw up all the courage she possessed to

knock on Ruth's door. Would she be accepted? Had the nurse and her two roommates already eaten and put away the food?

Before she could think another thought, the door of the house flew open and there stood Ruth, alpine tall with her arms outstretched like limbs of a redwood tree. "You've come!" she boomed, her two roommates looking on admiringly. "What an honor it is to have you for dinner."

"But . . . but," Nancy stammered, "surely the dinner is cold and . . . ."

"Of course! But we'll reheat it and have a wonderful time!" said Ruth as she led her guest to the table.[14]

The hostess saw in her mentoree that evening a girl who was reaching out for God, greatly confused about nearly every issue of doctrine between the pages of the sacred book. She followed Ruth everywhere—to the InterVarsity campground of Bear Trap Ranch in the mountains near Colorado Springs, to church on Sunday, and to Bible studies in Ruth's house. Eventually Nancy gave her heart to the Lord under Ruth's discipling, became a Marriage, Family, Child counselor, the mother of four children, and the wife of successful research engineer and entrepreneur, Jon Collins.

Ruth, who had ruled out matrimony, eventually married a widower and raised his three children, in addition to two children born of that union. It was she, ever the mentor, who took in the second son of Nancy and Jon at a needy point in his life, gave him a summer on her farm, and put him on the path to the Eternal City with her promise of faithful prayer.

There is nothing better than a home to serve as a base for mentoring. Ruth did what she could, and it was magnificent.

> They talk about a woman's sphere
>   as though it had a limit;
> There's not a place in earth or heaven,
> There's not a task to mankind given,
> There's not a blessing or a woe,
> There's not a whispered yes or no,
> There's not a life, or death, or birth,
> That has a feather's weight of worth —
>   without a woman in it.

In summary, the fruits of the Spirit represent love in its many forms. Since woman at her best represents love at its best, everyone in her presence sees more clearly what God wants them to be — the inheritors of a rich legacy from Him through His Son, Jesus Christ.

WHY MENTOR?

Scripture Paraphrased

Counsel in another's heart is like deep water, but a discerning man will draw it up.

> Proverbs 20:5

A straightforward answer is as good as a kiss of friendship.

> Proverbs 24:26

As iron sharpens iron, so one man sharpens the wit of another.

> Proverbs 27:17

EIGHT

JESUS CHRIST, THE DIVINE MENTOR

I am the way and the truth and the life. No one comes to the Father except through me.

John 14:6

N o mentor ever entered upon a mission as important as that of our Lord Jesus Christ. It is incredible that He who had at His disposal the very power of heaven and could have dazzled the angels as well as all mankind, would limit Himself to twelve humble men and through them work out His ministry. What kind of people did He entrust with His mission? How did He make His selection? How did He train them? Are there lessons here for the mentor today?

Robert Coleman comments on the choices Jesus made:

Jesus saw in these simple men the potential of leadership. They were indeed unlearned and ignorant from the world's standard but they were teachable. Though

often mistaken in their judgments and slow to comprehend spiritual things they were honest men, willing
to confess their need. Their mannerisms may have
been awkward and their abilities limited but with the
exception of the traitor, Judas, their hearts were big.
What is perhaps most significant about them is their
sincere yearning for God and the realities of His life.[1]

My friend and colleague Graeme Irvine, acting president of World Vision International, speculated that perhaps Jesus picked up His men at random ("Any twelve
will do!") in order to demonstrate the power of God to
transform and use any life. However, Irvine says, there is
scriptural evidence to suggest that our Lord chose His
men with great care.

It is worthy of note that before Jesus made His selection of twelve men, He spent the night in prayer. His
modus operandi was to immerse His men in the life and
work of the Kingdom of God. He did it by inviting them
to be with Him for the daily object lessons. He never said,
"Today, class, we will have a lesson on prayer. Please take
out your notebooks. Point one . . ." No, He taught His
mentorees by His life.

The Mentor Who Served

Christ's teaching went beyond pouring knowledge into
the heads of His disciples. It encompassed *values* as well.
This was not easy because the values He insisted on were
in sharp contrast to the values of that time, even though
the people of Israel had throughout their lifetimes a unique opportunity to know and obey the commandments of
God. Christ's men struggled constantly with Kingdom

values. It's the same today. What Jesus taught often seems backward, upside down, and just the reverse of what comes naturally.

Unlike mentors who are considered successful today, Jesus did not organize His team in order to be served. He never asked them to make Him look good. They were never required to wait on Him. Just the opposite was true: *He* served *them*. The Master built them up, encouraged them, corrected them, and stretched them as they struggled to receive the truth and obey the will of God. "Whoever wants to become great among you must be your servant," He taught in Mark 10:43–45, "and whoever wants to be first must be slave of all. For even the Son of Man did not come to be served, but to serve, and to give his life as a ransom for many." In John 13:15, He said in the upper room after washing their feet, "I have set you an example that you should do as I have done for you."

The Mentor Who Led

While stooping to serve, Jesus did not abandon His responsibilities as the leader. He reminded His disciples in the upper room, "You call me 'Teacher' and 'Lord,' and rightly so, for that is what I am" (John 13:13). He was not like the reluctant guide who says, "I must follow that group; I'm their leader!" Jesus remained an individual. When the disciples became so engrossed in His teaching of the five thousand by the sea that they forgot to eat, He was prepared. He knew exactly what to do. John is careful to point this out in chapter 6, verse 6 of his gospel. This clear sense of who He was is inspiring to us. It made more powerful His vested authority and strengthened His example of servant leadership.

The Mentor Who Was Vulnerable

The supreme Mentor did not hesitate to make Himself vulnerable. A leader who tries to integrate the values of the Kingdom of God will almost certainly be viewed by some as weak. A leader's natural temptation to react against this accusation is enormous. But look objectively at the person of Jesus and you will not be able to conclude that He was weak. His strength lay in His identity and purpose, not in the outward trappings of power, prestige, or force.

Constantly, Jesus was raising the sights of His band of disciples. He continually admonished them: "Lift up your eyes." He said it to His men after that remarkable conversation with the Samaritan woman recorded in John 4. When they did so, the disciples saw an entire village coming to Him because of her testimony. Jesus liked to steer against the status quo.

The Mentor of Both Genders

Jesus' attitude toward women illustrates graphically His ability to shake society loose from its prejudice and bigotry. Although there were no women among the twelve disciples, many among those who followed the twelve were women. To them, Christ accorded the full human dignity that was their rightful due and yet was universally denied by the society of New Testament times. He affirmed their characteristic gifts of insight, ministry, devotion, and courage — characteristics that often exceeded those of the twelve men themselves.

Toward the end of a three-year period of training, Jesus gathered His men into a tightening circle of intimacy and community. He called the disciples His friends, not His servants. Now and then He told them candidly that He was prepared to have His love tested by laying down His life for them. Some of the men matched Him point for point, but He told them frankly that such devotion would be strained to the limit.

In this context, Christ gave His disciples "a new commandment," a challenge to love one another as He had demonstrated. This was the recurring theme of the Master as He prepared to leave His devoted followers. He called it the highest expression of discipleship, easily recognized, often hard to embrace, but proof that a person characterized by love was indeed a follower of The Way. The Apostle John gives nearly a third of his gospel to the Lord's crowning theme — love — in the final days of His mission on earth.

The Mentor Who Trusted

In spite of the fact that the Lord knew most certainly that His little band would fail at critical times and in important issues, He was able to trust His assemblage of mentorees. To the question whether they were able to assume the work of the Kingdom, most of them would have responded with a resounding "No!" But He insisted that they could, and He prayed for them, loved them to the end, and entrusted to them His enormous and eternal undertaking. His command was simple: "Go and make disciples of all nations!" And in return, He said, they could count on receiving from God all of the resources they would need.

We are not protégés of Christ, of course, or mentorees in the strictest sense. And yet we would be wrong to call His life irrelevant in the light of His crucifixion and His resurrection with their deep theological significance. If Calvary were all that mattered, there would have been no point to Christ's thirty-three years of teaching and living and providing an example for His followers to emulate.

With Christ in Jerusalem

Join the Lord and His "mentors" as they walk through Jerusalem and note His method of teaching. The fourteenth chapter of the Gospel of Luke might be a good place to begin:

Verse 1: "*One Sabbath, when Jesus went to eat in the house of a prominent Pharisee, he was being carefully watched.*"

Wherever Jesus went, the eyes of the people were upon Him. His life was different, and He did not deny that He was the Author of a brand new way of life. John 10:10 records His words: "I have come that they may have life, and have it to the full." Because of these claims, people watched to see if He was genuine.

Our Lord was never caught doing something counter to what He taught. He lived by the principles He set forth, never by circumstances. Do you follow His example?

If you take your used car to the dealer to trade in for a new one and he asks if there is anything wrong with it, do you tell the truth?

If you are given more change at the check-out stand than you deserve, do you call it to the attention of the cashier?

If you owe money for which you are not billed, do you pay it anyhow?

A protégé of the divine Mentor lives by the principles taught by the Master.

Verse 2: *"There in front of him was a man suffering from dropsy."*

The Lord was constantly in touch with needy people. Everywhere He went they were "there in front of Him." Seldom did a needy person get turned down. He seemed to have denied the Syrophoenician woman, but eventually He met her need.

A protégé of the divine Mentor today is constantly in touch with people in need. Do you see the needy people around you?

As Jesus looked around in the house of one of the chief Pharisees, He noticed people elbowing their way to the best seats around the table. He used the situation to teach the following principle:

Verses 8–10: *"When someone invites you to a wedding feast, do not take the place of honor, for a person more distinguished than you may have been invited. If so, the host who invited both of you will come and say to you, 'Give this man your seat.' Then, humiliated, you will have to take the least important place. But when you are invited, take the lowest place, so that when your host comes, he will say to you, 'Friend, move up to a better place.' Then you will be honored in the presence of all your fellow guests."*

Jesus knows what is in the hearts of His mentorees. He wants to save them from embarrassment. He is providing instruction that will result in a person's feeling good rather than bad.

Is this graciousness a characteristic of your speaking to others?

Verse 11: *"For everyone who exalts himself will be humbled, and he who humbles himself will be exalted."*

Our appetites, desires, longings, and dreams are not wrong in themselves because God created them. They become wrong when we seek to satisfy them in an unscriptural way. In our scheming minds, we are sure that somehow it must be possible to *get* without *giving,* to be *first* without being *last,* and to *live* without *dying.* Do you encourage people to take God's way?

Verse 15: *"When one of those at the table with him heard this, he said to Jesus, 'Blessed is the man who will eat at the feast in the kingdom of God.'"*

Jesus took the opportunity to tell the story of a man who prepared a feast and invited all who were bidden. But they would not come, so the master of the house became angry and gathered up the poor, the maimed, the lame, and the blind to enjoy the dinner.

The story obviously refers to the kingdom of heaven and to that great feast with God the Father and the Lord Jesus Christ. Why would anyone reject an invitation to dine at God's table? Only if they did not know who was extending the invitation. The Apostle Paul provides some enlightenment: "None of the rulers of this age understood it, for if they had, they would not have crucified the Lord of glory" (1 Corinthians 2:8).

The Mentor's point is this: The Parable of the Great Supper reveals that a preoccupation with the insignificant makes it impossible to bring priorities into perspective. Rarely does the Spirit of God shout at a person. His voice usually comes in the form of a gentle prodding as the Scriptures are read. An obedient disciple is in tune with the Spirit of God.

Verse 25: *"Large crowds were traveling with Jesus."*

It's always been fashionable to speak a good word for Jesus Christ. A politican can garner votes by acting pious or quoting the Bible in his speeches. Gandhi, a devout Hindu, was an admirer of Jesus Christ. But note here in our text who it is that hears the Lord: "Now the tax collectors and 'sinners' were all gathering around to hear him" (Luke 15:1). The multitudes followed Him, but the publicans and sinners heard Him.

Jesus' message is designed for the desperate. It is for people who crave more than merely eking out an existence. They are the ones who "hear Him," who not only listen to what He says, but act on it.

One of the fundamental requisites for true discipleship is a spirit of desperation that burns deep within the soul.

Verse 26: *"If anyone comes to me and does not hate his father and mother, his wife and children, his brothers and sisters — yes, even his own life — he cannot be my disciple."*

Following the divine Mentor is costly. It begins with a willingness to renounce all other loyalties in preference to Jesus Christ. To be a disciple of Christ, I must follow Him and do His bidding even when it appears that it will cost me my mother and my father, my wife (or husband), and my children.

Verses 34–35: *"Salt is good, but if it loses its saltiness, how can it be made salty again? It is fit neither for the soil nor for the manure pile; it is thrown out. . . . "*

Jesus concludes His dissertation on discipleship by alluding to savorless salt. How does salt relate to discipling?

Walter A. Henrichsen, head of a discipling ministry for lay Christians in the business world, suggests that the parable is an illustration to the believer who refuses to be a disciple.

> It is God's design that every believer be a disciple. But when one goes back on his commitment, he becomes good for nothing. You can't save him; he is already saved. You can't use him; he is unavailable. He is like savorless salt. Men throw it out.[2]

For the mentoree who is worthy of the divine Mentor's investment in him, there is no turning back. It is only forward. In 1519 when Cortez landed at Vera Cruz to begin his dramatic conquest of Mexico with a handful of seven hundred men, he deliberately set fire to his fleet of eleven ships. His men on the shore watched helplessly as their only means of retreat sank to the bottom of the Gulf of Mexico. With their retreat gone, they had only one way to go—forward into the interior of Mexico for whatever lay in store.

You, too, must destroy all avenues of retreat. Determine in your heart that you will go wherever He sends, pay any price required, and enjoy the rewards of the true and the faithful.

A high-caste Hindu, who was one of the founding members of the Philosophical Society of India, a leader of Hindu Neo-Orthodoxy, and later became president of India, went to see Dr. S. Radhakrishnan. This man asked Dr. Radhakrishnan to be his guru.

Dr. Radhakrishnan said to him, "Young man, I am not worthy to be your guru."

"Well," said the caller, "if you are not worthy to be my guru, where should I find my guru?"

The reply was, "The only one I know of worthy to be your guru was Jesus Christ."

The Hindu snapped angrily, "How can you, a Brahmin, tell me, a Brahmin, that Jesus Christ can be my guru? Besides, He is dead. How could He be my guru?"

Dr. Radhakrishnan stroked his beard thoughtfully then responded, "Some of my very good friends insist to me that He is still alive."[3]

Let that intriguing response urge all Christian mentors to press on in their holy calling. Let each of us be prepared to "correct, rebuke, and encourage — with great patience and careful instruction" (2 Timothy 4:2) all those whom God has given us to serve.

SELECT BIBLIOGRAPHY

Alderfer, C. P. and L. David Brown. *Learning from Changing: Organizational Diagnosis and Development*. Beverly Hills, CA: Sage, 1975.

Atkinson et al. "Management Development Roles: Coach, Sponsor, and Mentor." *Personnel Journal* 59 (1980): 918–921.

Beckhard, R. and R. Harris. *Organizational Transitions*. Reading, MA: Addison-Wesley, 1977.

"Bendix Abuzz: Agee Shakes Up His Company." *Time* (October 6, 1980): 83.

Bird, C. *The Two Paycheck Marriage*. New York: Pocket Books, 1979.

Coppedge, Allan. *The Biblical Principles of Discipleship*. Grand Rapids, MI: Zondervan Publishing House, 1989.

Edman, V. Raymond. *The Disciplines of Life*. Minneapolis: World Wide Publications, 1948.

Getz, Gene. *Building Up One Another*. Wheaton, IL: Victor Books, 1976.

Hackman, J. R. and G. R. Oldham. *Work Redesign*. New York: Addison-Wesley, 1980.

Hackman, J. R. and J. L. Suttle. *Improving Life at Work*. Santa Monica: Goodyear, 1977.

Jepsen, Dee. *Women Beyond Equal Rights*. Dallas: Word Books, 1984.

Mason, Mike. *The Mystery of Marriage*. Portland: Multnomah Press, 1985.

Saranson, S. *Work, Ageing, and Social Change*. New York: Free Press, 1979.

Sofer, C. *Men in Mid-Career*. London: Cambridge University Press, 1970.

Watson, G. "Resistance to Change" in W. G. Bennis, K. F. Benae, and R. Chin (eds.). *The Planning of Change*. New York: Holt, Rinehart, and Winston, 1969.

Ziglar, Zig. *See You at the Top*. Dallas: Word Books, 1980.

END NOTES

INTRODUCTION

1. Judith Viorst, *Necessary Losses* (New York: Simon and Schuster, 1986), 179-180.

2. ANYONE CAN / EVERYONE SHOULD

1. John C. Maxwell, *Your Attitude: Key to Success* (San Bernardino, CA: Here's Life Publishers, Inc., 1984), 25.

2. Ibid., 25.

3. Viktor E. Frankl, *Man's Search for Meaning* (New York: Simon and Schuster, 1985), 85.

4. Lee Iaccoca and William Novak, *Iaccoca: An Autobiography* (New York: Bantam, 1984).

5. Personal letter to Ted Engstrom.

6. Helen Keller, *The Story of My Life* (New York: Doubleday, Page and Co., 1905), 311.

7. Mary Kay Ash, *People Management* (New York: Warner Books, 1984), 179.

8. Fred Smith, *You and Your Network* (Waco, TX: Word Books, 1984), 94.

9. Paul Borthwick, *Leading the Way* (Colorado Springs: Navpress, 1989), 168.

3. CALLING PROTÉGÉS TO ACCOUNT

1. Plato, *Dialogues, Apology* sec. 38.
2. Charles W. Colson, *Born Again* (Old Tappan, NJ, Chosen Books, 1976), 132.
3. Ibid., 146.
4. Personal letter to Ted Engstrom.

4. MENTORS IN THE HOME

1. Ingrid Trobisch, *The Joy of Being a Woman* (New York: Harper and Row, 1975), 13.
2. Quoted by Charles R. Swindoll, "Discipleship on Display", Audio cassette, First Evangelical Free Church, Fullerton, California.
3. Paul Borthwick, *Leading the Way* (Colorado Springs: Navpress, 1989), 24.
4. *Daily Guideposts* (May 1988): 141.

5. MENTORS IN THE CHURCH

1. Ralph Waldo Emerson, *The Conduct of Life* (1860).
2. Allan Coppedge, *The Biblical Principles of Discipleship* (Grand Rapids: Francis Asbury Press, 1989), 61.
3. Personal letter to Ted Engstrom.
4. Personal letter to Ted Engstrom.
5. Amy Carmichael, as quoted in J. Oswald Sanders, *Spiritual Leadership* (Chicago: Moody Press, 1967), 106.
6. Personal letter to Ted Engstrom.
7. Personal letter to Ted Engstrom.
8. Personal letter to Ted Engstrom.
9. C.S. Lewis, *The Four Loves* (London: Fontana, 1958), 138–139.
10 *Dipleship Journal*, Issue 41, (1987): 25.
11 Bill Hybels, *Who Are You When No One's Looking?* (Downers Grove, IL: InterVarsity Press, 1987), 64.
12 Ibid., 64.
13 Personal letter to Norman Rohrer.

14 Ibid.

6. VOCATIONAL MENTORS

1. Richard Halverson, *Perspective* (Grand Rapids: Zondervan, 1983).

2. "The Quest for Quality," Published by the Royal Bank of Canada, vol. 69, no. 6 (November/December 1988): 3

3. Ibid.

4. Lee Iaccoca and William Novak, *Iaccoca: An Autobiography* (New York: Bantam, 1984).

5. Mal King, *Mentoring: The Only Way to Develop Leaders* (unpublished manuscript).

6. Personal letter to Ted Engstrom.

7. Audio cassette, Conversation between Bobb Biehl and John Savage, chairman of the 1988 Leadership Institute under the Orange County United Way, Hispanic Development Council.

8. Ibid.

9. Mal King, *Mentoring: The Only Way to Develop Leaders* (unpublished manuscript).

10 Robert Coleman, *The Master Plan of Evangelism* (Old Tappan, NJ: Fleming H. Revell, 1968).

11 Ted W. Engstrom and Edward R. Dayton, *The Art of Management for Christian Leaders* (Dallas, TX: Word, 1982), 37.

12 Olan Hendrix, *Management for the Christian Worker* (Libertyville, IL: Quill Publications, 1976), 8.

13. Bruce W. Jones, *Ministerial Leadership in a Managerial World* (Weaton, IL: Tyndale, 1988).

14. Mal King, *Mentoring: The Only Way to Develop Leaders* (unpublished manuscript).

15. Personal communication to Norman Rohrer.

16. Charles R. Swindoll, "Discipleship on Display", Audio cassette, First Evangelical Free Church, Fullerton, California.

17. Ibid.

18. Personal letter to Ted Engstrom.

19. Mal King, *Mentoring: The Only Way to Develop Leaders* (unpublished manuscript).

20. Personal conversation with Norman Rohrer.

21. Kenneth A. Jolemore, Major General, U.S. Army, "More Than a Teacher, More Than a Coach: Traditional Mentoring in the Military," *Military Review*, (1986), USACGSC, Ft. Leavenworth, Kansas.

22. Martin Blumenson, *The Patton Papers, 1885–1940* (Boston: Houghton Mifflin Co., 1972), 13.

23. Excerpted from Fred Smith, *You and Your Network* (Dallas, TX: Word Books, 1984), 105–116.

24. George MacDonald, *Mary Marston*.

7. WOMEN AS MENTORS

1. Quoted by Edith Deen, *The Bible's Legacy for Womanhood* (Old Tappan, NJ: Fleming H. Revell, Spire Books Division, 1976), 8.

2. Dee Brestin, *The Friendships of Women* (Wheaton, IL: Victor Books, 1988).

3. Edith Deen, *The Bible's Legacy for Womanhood* (Old Tappan, NJ: Fleming H. Revell, Spire Books Division, 1976), 7.

4. Edith Deen, *The Bible's Legacy for Womanhood* (Old Tappan, NJ: Fleming H. Revell, Spire Books Division, 1976).

5. Nancy W. Collins, *Professional Women and Their Mentors* (Englewood Cliffs, NJ: Prentice-Hall, 1983).

6. Mal King, *Mentoring: The Only Way to Develop Leaders* (unpublished manuscript).

7. Ibid., (epilogue).

8. Gail Sheehy, "The Mentor Connection: The Secret Link in the Successful Woman's Life," *New York Magazine* (April 5, 1976).

9. Linda Phillips-Jones, *Mentors and Protégés* (New York: Arbor House, 1982), 37.

10 Dee Brestin, *The Friendships of Women* (Wheaton, IL: Victor Books, 1988), 151.

11 Dee Brestin, *The Friendships of Women* (Wheaton, IL: Victor Books, 1988).

12 Karen Mains, "An Interview with Karen Mains: Our Search for Spiritual Mentors," *Virtue* (October 1985), 73.

13 Personal letter to Ted Engstrom.

14 Personal communication with Norman Rohrer.

8. JESUS CHRIST, THE DIVINE MENTOR

1. Robert Coleman, *The Master Plan of Evangelism* (Old Tappan, NJ: Fleming H. Revell, 1968).

2. Walter A. Henrichsen, *Disciples Are Made, Not Born* (Wheaton, IL: Victor Books, 1988), 40.

3. Personal letter to Ted Engstrom.

ABOUT THE
AUTHOR

A s the former president and chief executive officer of World Vision (and now President Emeritus) and a director on numerous boards, Ted W. Engstrom is one of the most influential leaders in American religion and social service. He has been the recipient of three honorary doctorates (L.H.D., Taylor University; LL.D., John Brown University, and Litt.D., Seattle Pacific University).

Before joining World Vision, Engstrom was for six years president of Youth for Christ International. He is a sought-after management consultant and has conducted the nationwide "Managing Your Time" seminars with his colleague Ed Dayton for more than fourteen years.

A prolific editor and author, Engstrom has written forty books and hundreds of magazine articles. Among his most recent books are *The Pursuit of Excellence* (Zondervan), *The Fine Art of Friendship* (Nelson), and *Integrity* (Word).

As President Emeritus of World Vision, Dr. Engstrom continues with a full load of speaking, writing, and leadership training.

The typeface for the text of this book is *Goudy Old Style*. Its creator, Frederic W. Goudy, was commissioned by American Type Founders Company to design a new Roman type face. Completed in 1915 and named Goudy Old Style, it was an instant bestseller. However, its designer had sold the design outright to the foundry, so when it became evident that additional versions would be needed to complete the family, the work was done by the foundry's own designer, Morris Benton. From the original design came seven additional weights and variants, all of which sold in great quantity. However, Goudy himself received no additional compensation for them. He later recounted a visit to the foundry with a group of printers, during which the guide stopped at one of the busy casting machines and stated, "Here's where Goudy goes down to posterity, while American Type Founders Company goes down to prosperity."

Substantive Editing:
Michael S. Hyatt

Copy Editing:
Susan Kirby

Cover Design:
Kent Puckett Associates, Atlanta, Georgia

Page Composition:
Xerox Ventura Publisher
Printware 720 IQ Laser Printer

Printing and Binding:
Maple-Vail Book Manufacturing Group,
York, Pennsylvania

Dust Jacket Printing:
Weber Graphics, Chicago, Illinois